W9-BNC-085

DISCARD

BOOKS BY ERNEST R. MAY

AMERICAN IMPERIALISM

A Speculative Essay

AMERICAN IMPERIALISM

A Speculative Essay

ERNEST R. MAY

ATHENEUM

New York

1968

Previously published in different form in *Perspectives in American History*, Volume 1 (1967), by the Charles Warren Center for Studies in American History, Harvard University

Copyright © 1967, 1968 by Ernest R. May
All rights reserved
Library of Congress catalog card number 68–12544
Published simultaneously in Canada by McClelland and Stewart Ltd.
Manufactured in the United States of America by H. Wolff, New York
Designed by Kathleen Carey
First Edition

For Nancy

PREFACE

SOME YEARS AGO I produced a book on the emergence of the United States as a great power. It dealt chiefly with changes in American behavior toward other states during the 1890s and consequent changes in European ideas about America's place in international politics. Reviewing it for the New York *Herald Tribune,* Carl Degler commented not unkindly that it skirted discussion of movement within the United States that might account for altered conduct abroad.

Though believing that one writes a book in order to forget a subject, I saw the truth of Degler's comment. It never quite left my mind. An invitation to edit some documents on American imperialism caused me to face it frontally. Though the documentary collection did not materialize, a draft of an introductory essay grew into a paper for the Massachusetts Historical Society; the paper became a book-length essay, entitled "American Imperialism: A Reinterpretation," which appeared in the first issue of the Charles Warren Center's annual *Perspectives in American History;* and the essay, considerably revised, becomes this book.

It does not entirely answer Degler's point. Indeed, it deals with only one of Degler's many implicit questions: Why did American public opinion swing around during the 1890s on the subject of whether or not the United States should possess a colonial empire? But that simple-seeming question hides puzzles enough to provoke more than one book.

Historians have said much about public opinion as the molder of American foreign policy. Few, however, have attempted to explain how policy-makers heard the public, or pretended to hear it, or made it speak. Fewer still have anatomized the publics to which policy-makers listened or analyzed how opinions gestated within them. Thomas A. Bailey's *The Man in the Street,* the only book by a historian that inspects these topics, appeared in 1948, when scientific understanding of public opinion gave pollsters confidence in Thomas E. Dewey. Since then political scientists, sociologists, and psychologists have discarded many once accepted premises and developed much more reliable models of public opinion and its behavior. This essay makes use of recent social science findings. It does not pretend to test or prove them. At most it may lead other historians to reexamine other episodes and suggest to students of the present-day scene perceptions they might discover by looking backward. Certainly this work will not stand as a permanent answer to the historical question on which it focuses. Comments from Morton Keller, Walter LaFeber, Arthur Mann, H. Douglas Price, and Robert Zenowich have already caused me to revise substantially the version published in

Perspectives. Had I paid more attention to these friends or waited for criticism from others, the book might show many more changes. But it is meant to provoke rather than to satisfy. The sooner it becomes obsolete, the more successful it will have been.

Apart from those who provided helpful criticism, there are many to whom I owe debts: Ralph Tyler and the trustees of the Center for Advanced Study in the Behavioral Sciences, for a contemplative fellowship year with colleagues from a mixture of disciplines; the staffs of the Harvard, Columbia, Berkeley, and Stanford libraries, the Boston and New York public libraries, the Library of Congress, and the Massachusetts Historical Society, for making available research materials; the trustees of the Henry P. Kendall Foundation, for grants that permitted photocopying and employment of research assistants; Bernard Bailyn and Donald H. Fleming, the editors of *Perspectives,* for encouraging publication of the earlier version; the director, the administrative committee, and the staff of the Charles Warren Center for the Study of American History, for a travel grant and typing service; Diana Meister, for preparing, proofreading, and collating three versions and, above all, seeing to it that students, colleagues, and callers did not prevent writing; three children, for being tolerant of a preoccupied father; and my wife, Nancy, for having the good judgment to insist that I make sense to someone more interested in English literature than in social science.

Belmont, Massachusetts
JULY 12, 1967

CONTENTS

AMERICAN IMPERIALISM

A Speculative Essay

I

SOME ANSWERS AND
SOME QUESTIONS

IN 1898–99 THE United States suddenly became a colonial power. It annexed the Hawaiian Islands. Humbling Spain in a short war, it took Puerto Rico and the Philippines. In quick sequence it also acquired Guam and part of Samoa and, if the Danish Rigsdag had consented, would have bought the Virgin Islands. In an eighteen-month period it became master of empires in the Caribbean and the Pacific.

Viewing America's tradition as anticolonial, historians have found these events puzzling. The legislative resolution for war with Spain seemingly expressed this tradition. Calling for independence for Spain's Cuban colony, Congress disclaimed "any disposition or intention to exercise sovereignty, jurisdiction, or control over" Cuba. That the same body should have ended the war by annexing Puerto Rico

3

and Spanish islands in the Pacific appears a paradox, and many historians see 1898–99 as, in Samuel Flagg Bemis' phrase, a "great aberration."

To be sure, Americans of the time were hustled along by events. The first battle of the war took place not in Cuba but in Spain's more distant Philippine colony. A spectacular success, in which Admiral Dewey's squadron overcame all opposition without losing a single ship or life, it surprised many Americans into their first awareness that the Philippine Islands existed and that Spain owned them. Soon, however, following reports that Dewey's victory had shaken Spain's control, American troops sailed to seize the colonial capital, Manila. On the ground that these troops would need a support base in mid-Pacific, Congress annexed the Hawaiian Islands. By war's end, therefore, the United States already had one Pacific colony, and debate centered on whether to acquire another in the Philippines.

Both Americans and Europeans assumed that the United States could dispose of the Philippines as it chose. Seeming alternatives included handing the islands back to Spain, arranging for transfer to a European power, insisting on independence, or annexing. Most Americans saw the first alternative as giving up a hard-won prize and, moreover, returning the Filipinos to virtual slavery; the second as throwing an apple of discord among European states, perhaps even leading to general war; and the third, given the low level of Philippine development, as infeasible. Annexation appeared the least unattractive course.[1]

[1] In the abundant literature on these decisions, see, in addition to the

American politicians could reason so, however, only by assuming that annexation would not cost votes at home. The historical puzzle rises from the fact that politicians then in power apparently did not expect to pay a price at the polls. Why not? With anticolonialism as strong as the Congressional war resolution suggests, how could politicians conclude that a colonialist policy could safely be pursued?

In *Expansionists of 1898* Julius W. Pratt offers part of an answer.[2] He shows that, after Dewey's victory, religious journals changed tone. The Baptist *Standard*, the Presbyterian *Interior* and *Evangelist*, the Congregationalist *Advance*, and the *Catholic World* all spoke of rule over the Philippines as America's Christian duty. Methodist, Episcopalian, and Campbellite organs said the same. Only Quaker and Unitarian papers stood unitedly in opposition.

Pratt also shows the business press following a similar pattern. Having in the past either opposed or said nothing about acquisition of new territory, business journals now

---

works discussed later in this chapter, my own *Imperial Democracy: The Emergence of America as a Great Power* (New York, 1961), Margaret Leech, *In the Days of McKinley* (New York, 1959), H. Wayne Morgan, *William McKinley and His America* (Syracuse, 1963), and William A. Russ, Jr., *The Hawaiian Revolution, 1893–1894* and *The Hawaiian Republic, 1894–1898* (Selinsgrove, Pa., 1959 and 1961). Lesser episodes in American expansion are discussed in Earl S. Pomeroy, *Pacific Outpost: American Strategy in Guam and Micronesia* (Stanford, Calif., 1951), George Herbert Ryden, *The Foreign Policy of the United States in Relation to Samoa* (New Haven, 1933), Charles Callan Tansill, *The Purchase of the Danish West Indies* (Baltimore, 1932), and Alfred Vagts, *Deutschland und die Vereinigten Staaten in der Weltpolitik*, 2 vols. (New York, 1935), I, 641–738, II, 1321–1524.

[2] Julius W. Pratt, *Expansionists of 1898: The Acquisition of Hawaii and the Spanish Islands* (Baltimore, 1936), pp. 230–316.

5

talked of the advantages of expansion. The New York *Journal of Commerce* came out for Hawaiian annexation even before the war started. After Dewey's victory others followed suit, with a number also speaking for a permanent coaling station in the Philippines or even annexation of the whole archipelago. Pratt cites editorials in the *Wall Street Journal*, the *United States Investor*, the *Financial Record*, *Bradstreet's*, the New York *Commercial*, the *American Banker*, the *Banker and Tradesman*, the *Age of Steel*, and *Iron Age*. Some of these editorials expressed reservations, to be sure; a few journals resisted the trend, notably the widely read *Commercial and Financial Chronicle;* and some observers described businessmen as being generally non-committal.[3] By and large, nevertheless, religious and business periodicals both registered approval of colonial expansion.

Before finally making up his mind, President McKinley toured the Midwest. Standing before large audiences, he delivered equivocal speeches. Some lines hinted at a decision to annex the Philippines; other lines hinted the opposite. His staff took notes on the relative levels of applause and reported that proannexation words drew louder handclaps.[4] Other public figures presumably had similar experiences. Politicians thus had before them persuasive evidence of a

---

[3] The New York *Journal of Commerce,* though itself expansionist, commented regretfully on Aug. 29, 1898, on the "deathlike silence" of most of the business community. See also Charles G. Dawes to McKinley, Aug. 10, 1898, and James Ford Rhodes to McKinley, Sept. 28, 1898, Private Papers of William McKinley, Manuscripts Division, Library of Congress.

[4] See May, *Imperial Democracy,* pp. 258–259.

6

dramatic swing in public opinion.

Such evidence explains their behavior partly but not entirely. In the past they had had plenty of evidence of antiexpansionist feeling. Though knowing in 1890 that minor tariff changes could encourage Canadians to seek annexation, congressmen found so little public enthusiasm that they failed to enact the changes.[5] When voting the war resolution, they evidently felt that the people would not want Cuba. One might suppose that politicians would have anticipated the public's recovery from a momentary fancy for Pacific colonies and its repudiation of the officeholders who had pandered to such a perversion. That politicians showed no such fear must mean that they had some basis for believing the whim would endure. They must have seen some impulse stronger than momentary excitement over victories in far-off places. What can it have been? What conditions existed conducive to a lasting popular movement in favor of imperialism?

This question has challenged historians. Setting aside versions that stress Providence, the westward trend, or inherent tendencies in capitalism, one can single out four major efforts to answer it. Each emphasizes a different factor.

Frederick Merk, the preeminent historian of American expansion in the 1840s, argues that a long-lived Manifest Destiny tradition offset the anticolonial tradition.[6] In *Mani-*

[5] Donald F. Warner, *The Idea of Continental Union: Agitation for the Annexation of Canada to the United States, 1849–1893* (Lexington, Ky., 1960), pp. 163–238.

[6] Frederick Merk, *Manifest Destiny and Mission in American History: A Reinterpretation* (New York, 1963), pp. 228–266.

fest Destiny and Mission in American History he describes two schools of thought existing at the time of the Mexican War. One, he says, favored the acquisition of territory in order to increase the nation's wealth and power. The other laid more stress on America's mission as the exemplar of democracy and individual liberty. After the victories of Taylor and Scott, men in the first school favored taking all or most of Mexico. Those in the second school wanted only sparsely inhabited tracts which settlers could easily turn into other Kentuckys and Ohios. In an epilogue on the 1890s Merk suggests that the ideas of the first, or Manifest Destiny, school reappeared later as imperialism, while the idea of Mission persisted as anti-imperialism. The two traditions had had equal hardihood, and the circumstances of 1898–99 gave the expansionist tradition an edge.

Explaining the actions of McKinley and other politicians would be an awareness of the expansionist tradition and an assumption that the balance had tipped toward it and away from the tradition of Mission. For parallels one might think of politicians concluding in 1913 that the protectionist tradition had lost out to the free-trade tradition or, in 1964, that states' rights had lost out to civil rights. In Merk's view the Manifest Destiny tradition provides the key to understanding what happened in 1898–99.

Julius Pratt emphasizes Social Darwinism. In *Expansionists of 1898* and elsewhere Pratt describes the expansionism of the 1890s as having a different rationale from that of pre-Civil War days.[7] It took from Herbert Spencer and other

7 Julius W. Pratt, "The 'Large Policy' of 1898," *Mississippi Valley His-*

writers the idea of an endless struggle testing each nation's fitness to survive. On this premise the United States had to seize whatever share of the earth it could, for not to do so would give advantages to rivals and in the long run would lead to defeat, decay, and decline. Expansion presented itself not as an open choice but as a necessity dictated by stern scientific law.

The premise already had wide acceptance. Dealing with domestic economic and social issues, writers and clergymen commonly invoked such formulae as "struggle for survival" and "survival of the fittest." At an early point some Americans progressed to conclusions about how the United States should behave internationally. Pointing to the navy's shift from sail to steam, they argued that the United States would stand at a dangerous disadvantage without coaling stations in distant seas. The Spanish War then created opportunities for acquiring such stations, far out in the Pacific as well as in the Caribbean. It also placed in America's grasp territories which, if not seized, could go to potential rivals. And it offered a seeming chance for Protestant Christianity (also a species, by Social Darwinist canons) to score a gain in its struggle for survival against Catholicism and heathenism. In Pratt's view these Social Darwinist theses captured American public opinion. The anticolonial tradition would not have intimidated politicians, because they would have expected these new ideas to dominate future public think-

torical Review, XIX (Sept. 1932), 219–242. See also Pratt's "The Ideology of American Expansion," in Avery Craven, ed., Essays in Honor of William E. Dodd by His Former Students at the University of Chicago (Chicago, 1935), pp. 335–353.

9

ing about foreign policy.

In *The New Empire,* a more recent book than either Merk's or Pratt's, Walter LaFeber stresses economic forces.[8] Like Pratt, he regards post-Civil War expansionism as different from that of the prewar era, but different because businessmen now captained the country and set their sights on markets rather than land. Whether manufacturers, merchants, or investors, they feared lest America's multiplying factories produce more than Americans could buy. As European states laid on protective tariffs, their thoughts turned to colonies and spheres of influence. Politicians behaved as they did in the 1890s, LaFeber suggests, because they put the interests of business ahead of all else, assumed the electorate would do the same, judged colonial expansion to serve business, and counted on the public's coming to the same conclusion and endorsing their actions.

A fourth major interpretation of the period, that of Richard Hofstadter, describes expansionism as merely one manifestation of a widespread "psychic crisis." [9] The rise of bigger, more powerful, and more bureaucratized business organizations produced protest in strikes such as those at Homestead and Pullman and political movements such as those of the Populists and Bryanite Democrats. These forms of protest failed. Meanwhile, with such savants as

[8] Walter LaFeber, *The New Empire: An Interpretation of American Expansion, 1860–1898* (Ithaca, 1963).

[9] Richard Hofstadter, "Manifest Destiny and the Philippines," in Daniel Aaron, ed., *America in Crisis* (New York, 1952), pp. 173–200, and *The Paranoid Style in American Politics and Other Essays* (New York, 1966), pp. 145–187.

Frederick Jackson Turner warning that the free land frontier no longer existed to drain off the discontented, members of the urban middle class took alarm not only at the
growth of big business but at the radicalism of the protest-
ers. For Americans in all these groups, Hofstadter argues,
war with Spain and annexation of distant islands represented an escape from reality—madcap behavior comparable to that of disturbed adolescents. Politicians presumably
counted on the public's remaining in this state of mind and
applauding the acquisition of new frontiers rather than
swinging back to disapproval of expansion.

The interpretations of Merk, Pratt, LaFeber, and Hofstadter can be reconciled. One could picture LaFeber's
businessmen as borrowers of the Manifest Destiny tradition, differing from expansionists of the 1840s in questing
for consumers rather than resources and quoting Herbert
Spencer instead of the Book of Genesis, and one could explain their success in the 1890s as due to the "psychic crisis." But even such a blend of interpretations leaves two
questions unanswered.

The first has to do with process. Merk does not say how
the Manifest Destiny tradition came temporarily to
outbalance the tradition of Mission. Pratt does not show
how the Social Darwinist prescription won acceptance. La-
Feber fails to explain how businessmen came to see expansion as in their interest. Hofstadter offers no reason why
men caught in a "psychic crisis" concluded that Pacific
islands would be good things to have. No one charts the
phases through which the individuals making up the public

might have passed as they changed their convictions about colonies.

The second open question has to do with timing. Why did the change take place when it did?

Through the 1870s and 1880s the tradition of Mission, as Merk interprets it, appeared to hold the field. The influence of Social Darwinism did not extend to thought about foreign policy, and businessmen gave few signs of seeing colonial expansion as an answer to overproduction.[10] At the end of the eighties, reports that Germany was about to take over Samoa produced some discussion of America's interest in the islands. Though no one spoke as a full-fledged expansionist, not everyone adopted the doctrinaire view that the United States could not consider taking part of the archipelago.

When Americans in Hawaii overthrew the native ruler in 1893 and appealed for annexation by the United States, politicians and newspaper reporters detected a surprising degree of public support for such a step. Some historians have concluded that if President Grover Cleveland had been of a mind to acquire the islands, he could have carried Congress and the country with him.[11] Thus, despite the public's show

[10] See Richard Hofstadter, *Social Darwinism in American Thought* (New York, 1944), Henry F. May, *The Protestant Churches and Industrial America* (New York, 1949), and Sidney Fine, *Laissez-Faire and the General Welfare State: A Study of Conflict in American Thought, 1865–1901* (Ann Arbor, Mich., 1956).

[11] Russ, *Hawaiian Revolution*, pp. 143–155; May, *Imperial Democracy*, pp. 13–24. The Samoan debates are in 50 Cong., 2 sess., *Congressional Record*, pp. 108–109, 1283–91, 1433–41. See also Charles Callan Tansill, *The Foreign Policy of Thomas F. Bayard, 1885–1897* (New York, 1940), pp. 68–122, and Vagts, *Deutschland und die Vereinigten Staaten*, I, 636–938.

of disinterest in annexing Canada and despite the language in Congress' 1898 war resolution, some shift away from anticolonialism could be observed even before Dewey's victory and its sequel. Circumstances created by the war will not account entirely for the estimates of public opinion formed by McKinley and other politicians. One has to ask why an apparent change in public attitudes should have set in around the beginning of the nineties.

Merk does not deal with this question. Pratt does so only indirectly. Describing books and essays by Josiah Strong, John Fiske, John W. Burgess, Alfred Thayer Mahan, and Henry Cabot Lodge that appeared after 1885, he implies that these writings had continuing and growing influence.[12] LaFeber has at least a partial answer. According to his reconstruction, the idea of colonial expansion as a partial solution to overproduction gained ground after 1879, when European states began putting up protective tariffs, and became much more attractive when the domestic market suddenly shrank in the panic of 1893. Hofstadter responds to the question by saying, in effect, that the turn to expansionism originated in the "psychic crisis" and that, since the

[12] Pratt, *Expansionists of 1898*, pp. 1–22. The works in question are Josiah Strong, *Our Country: Its Possible Future and Its Present Crisis* (New York, 1885); John Fiske, "Manifest Destiny," in *Harper's New Monthly Magazine*, LXX (March 1885), 578–590, and in Fiske's *American Political Ideas Viewed from the Standpoint of Universal History* (New York, 1885), pp. 101–152; John W. Burgess, *Political Science and Comparative Constitutional Law*, 2 vols. (Boston, 1890); Alfred Thayer Mahan, *The Influence of Sea Power upon History, 1660–1783* (Boston, 1890), and articles collected in *The Interest of America in Sea Power, Present and Future* (Boston, 1897); and Henry Cabot Lodge, "Our Blundering Foreign Policy," *Forum*, XIX (March 1895), 8–17.

"psychic crisis" occurred in the 1890s, it could only have come at that time.

But the timing of American imperialism has an aspect that neither LaFeber nor Hofstadter adequately explains. Change occurred after 1898 as well as before. After annexing the Philippines and negotiating treaties for acquisition of part of Samoa and all of the Danish West Indies, McKinley stood for reelection. He won by a larger margin than in 1896, in a contest characterized by his Democratic opponent as a referendum on imperialism. After his assassination in 1901 the presidency went to Vice President Theodore Roosevelt, who had been an ardent champion of colonial expansion. Yet the United States did not continue a career as an imperial power.

Not only did the American government make no efforts after 1900 to acquire new islands in the Caribbean or Pacific, it deliberately spurned opportunities to do so. Theodore Roosevelt rebuffed Haitians and Dominicans who dropped proannexation hints, and during nearly eight years as President he acquired only one piece of real estate—the ten-mile-wide Canal Zone in Panama. Though one may cite the Platt Amendment, as applied to Cuba, the acquisition of the Canal Zone, and the Roosevelt Corollary to the Monroe Doctrine as evidence that the United States still had a mild case of imperialism, the nation's expansion as a colonial power effectively came to an end as of 1899 or 1900.

After that date, moreover, politicians reverted to the working assumption they had employed before 1898. McKinley and Roosevelt took it for granted that public opinion would not approve keeping Cuba as a colony. They

judged that acquisition of a leasehold in China or annexation of Haiti, Santo Domingo, or a portion of Central
America would be unpopular. And no evidence contradicted these judgments. After 1900 scarcely a congressman
or newspaper editor raised his voice in favor of further colonial extension. Imperialism as a current in American public opinion appeared to be dead.[13]

None of the theories concerning the rise of the imperial-

---

[13] William Appleman Williams, *The Tragedy of American Diplomacy*,
rev. ed. (New York, 1962), contends that business-centered American
governments developed a strategy of "open door imperialism." Resembling British policy in the early nineteenth century, this strategy assumed American competitive superiority. [See John Gallagher and Ronald E. Robinson, "The Imperialism of Free Trade," *Economic History
Review*, 2nd Ser., VI (Aug. 1953), 1–15.] Instead of seeking, like European powers, to shut other nations out of colonial areas, the United States
worked only to insure that Americans were not excluded. Although this
goal sometimes required acquisition of islands, since bases were needed
both for trade and for the exercise of political and military influence, it
did not require assumption of larger administrative responsibilities. Americans, by their competitive superiority, could achieve economic domi-
nance without taking on such burdens. According to this line of reasoning, the change after 1900 is almost insignificant, for decisions on whether
or not to annex particular islands became, in effect, tactical decisions.
The grand strategy of American imperialism remained unaltered. Obviously the present study not only has different points of departure but
also different premises. This essay assumes that political behavior consists of an aggregate of individual actions influenced by diverse factors
and therefore seldom if ever comprehensible in terms of any pervasive
underlying purpose. But, in addition, there is a surface difference which
makes it unnecessary here to pursue more basic issues. This work deals
with imperialism narrowly defined as direct territorial acquisition and
with the question of why that particular form of political behavior ceased.
The subject matter of the essay is thus much narrower than that of Williams' book. It is also narrower than that of William E. Leuchtenburg's
celebrated essay, "Progressivism and Imperialism: The Progressive Movement and American Foreign Policy, 1898–1916," *Mississippi Valley Historical Review*, XXXIX (Dec. 1952), 483–504, in which imperialism
embraces actions asserting American supremacy in the Western Hemisphere.

ist movement satisfactorily explains its sudden demise. While Merk may be right that, over the long term, Mission had more power than Manifest Destiny, such a hypothesis does not in itself explain why, in this instance, Manifest Destiny enjoyed such short-lived ascendancy. Social Darwinism, the factor stressed by Pratt, had as much currency in 1902 as in 1898, yet seemed not to work the same effect on thought about foreign policy. LaFeber's businessmen had the same standing as before and regarded overproduction with only a little, if any, less concern. No apparent economic factor would account for their having different feelings about colonies. If a "psychic crisis" actuated imperialism, then it must have been literally a crisis, followed by quick recovery.

None of these comments depreciates the work of Merk, Pratt, LaFeber, and Hofstadter: all historians leave some questions unanswered. Nor does the present essay pretend to prove any of the four wrong. To the factors they have stressed, it adds a fifth—the impact on Americans of English and European examples. It does not, however, assert that this influence dominated. As much synthesis as reinterpretation, this study endeavors to portray the public that would have had opinion about expansion and to indicate how tradition, Social Darwinism, market hunger, psychological turmoil, *and* awareness of foreign fashions combined to cause a shift away from the anticolonial tradition at about the beginning of the 1890s, an upsurge of genuine imperialism in 1898–99, and then an abrupt return to the earlier faith.

16

II

THE STRUCTURE OF
PUBLIC OPINION

WHEN WE SAY that during the 1890s the American public changed its mind about colonies, what do we mean? Concerned with the public to which politicians reacted ("effective public opinion," in Herbert Blumer's phrase[1]), we must refer not to the population at large but to the voting public.

As of the 1890s fewer than 20 per cent of Americans voted. With the total population between 65.6 and 76 million, the presidential elections of 1892, 1896, and 1900 saw voting turnouts of 12 to 14 million. Though some wives dictated to husbands and though others who could not vote

---

[1] Herbert Blumer, "Public Opinion and Public Opinion Polling," in Bernard Berelson and Morris Janowitz, eds., *Reader in Public Opinion and Communication,* rev. ed. (Glencoe, Ill., 1953), pp. 594–602.

undoubtedly had influence, the public watched by politicians cannot have exceeded 13–15 million. Including no minors or Indians, few women, fewer unnaturalized immigrants, and only a small proportion of Negroes, this public did not reproduce the characteristics of the public portrayed by the census. It probably did not even represent white males over twenty-one.

The mid-twentieth-century voting public, at least in presidential years, contains more businessmen or professional men than clerical workers, more clerical workers than skilled workers, more skilled workers than farmers, and more farmers than unskilled workers. The following table shows the disparities:

Percentage of Eligible Voters Voting in Presidential Elections

FROM HOUSEHOLD HEADED BY:	AVG., 1948–60	PEAK YEAR (1952)
Business or professional men	76	88
Clerical workers	74	81
Skilled workers	68	74
Farmers	65	67
Unskilled workers	53	60

Contemporary surveys find voting turnout in the highest income group to be twelve times that in the lowest. Also, finding college graduates more apt to vote than high school graduates and high school graduates much more apt to vote than men or women with only grade school education, they

18

report certain occupational, income, and education-level groups to be overrepresented in the voting public.[2]

The nineteenth-century voting public no doubt differed from today's. Among those entitled to vote, turnout ran much higher: in presidential years, over 75 per cent nationally and well over 80 per cent in Northern and Western states, where whites made less effort to keep Negroes from the polls; in off years, above the present-day rate for presidential years.[3]

Also, the population and the electorate contained a far higher proportion of farmers. As the following table indicates, farmers and farm workers accounted for perhaps a third of the nation's working force:

Occupational Group	Percentage of Total Gainfully Employed	
	1950	*1900*
Business/Professional	17.3	10.1
Clerical	19.3	7.5
Skilled	42.4	26.9
Farm operators	7.4	19.9
Unskilled (incl. farm)	13.5	35.6

Farmers apparently turned out in large numbers. Walter Dean Burnham reports "awesome rates," sometimes ex-

[2] Robert E. Lane, *Political Life: Why and How People Get Involved in Politics* (Glencoe, Ill., 1959), p. 48.

[3] Walter Dean Burnham, "The Changing Shape of the American Political Universe," *American Political Science Review*, LIX (March 1965), 10–11.

ceeding 90 per cent, for primarily rural states such as Indiana and Iowa.[4] A crude sample from the latter state suggests a trifle higher rate among nonfarm rural dwellers than among actual farmers. In three Iowa counties (Adair, Audubon, and Davis) numbers of families primarily engaged in agriculture ran over 70 per cent. In three others (Dubuque, Polk, and Scott) the figure fell below 20 per cent. In voting-age populations, numbers of foreign born, and other possible distorting elements, the six counties resembled one another. In the 1900 presidential election, voting turnout averaged 22.2 per cent of the total population in the three predominantly agricultural counties, 22.5 in the other three.[5] By interpolation, one can calculate a turnout ratio of 21.1 per cent for the agricultural and 22.8 per cent for the nonagricultural population. Still, farmers in the 1890s would seem to have voted almost as faithfully as businessmen and professional men.

Given the high average turnout rate, the voting public probably contained 4 to 4.5 million farmers, nearly all of the nation's 2 to 2.5 million businessmen and professional men, and most of the 1.5 million males classified as clerical and sales workers. The 20 per cent of the labor force owning or operating farms, in other words, cast a third of the

[4] *Ibid.*, p. 16.

[5] Population data from Iowa Executive Council, *Census of Iowa for the Year 1905* (Des Moines, 1905); election data from the *World Almanac and Encyclopedia, 1902* (New York, 1902). For impressionistic evidence of a fairly high level of political interest in agricultural communities see T. N. Carver, "Life in the Corn Belt," *The World's Work*, VII (Dec. 1903), 4232–39, and Gustav P. Warber, "Social and Economic Survey of a Community in Northeastern Minnesota," *Bulletin of the University of Michigan* (March 1915).

vote; the 10 per cent in business or the professions cast 15 to 16 per cent; the 10 per cent in white collar jobs, 10 to 12 per cent. The nation's 12 to 14 million skilled and unskilled workers accounted for the remaining 4.5 to 5.5 million votes. Even if a third were minors or immigrants ineligible to vote, workers—and unskilled workers most of all—must have been underrepresented and men of higher than average income and education overrepresented.

Of course the voting public subdivided into many special publics. Statements about public opinion on colonies cannot refer to the whole voting public any more than to the whole population, but only to that portion specially interested. Though the subject may have attracted some citizens who did not usually pay attention to international affairs, this special public probably overlapped with what today we would call the foreign policy public.

Despite the frequency of crises in recent years, post-World War II survey data show this foreign policy public to be relatively small. In the years 1945 to 1949, despite the onset of the Cold War, the Truman Doctrine, the Marshall Plan, the Berlin blockade, the North Atlantic Treaty, the Soviet detonation of an atomic bomb, and Communist take-over in China, pollsters consistently found 30 per cent of the population unaware of any problems in foreign policy, another 45 per cent aware but totally uninformed, and only 25 per cent with both awareness and rudimentary knowledge.[6]

These figures described the adult population, not the vot-

[6] Lester Markel *et al., Public Opinion and Foreign Policy* (New York, 1949), pp. 49–56.

ing public. Interpreting them, one has to bear in mind this fact along with the fact that people do not necessarily need information to hold opinions. Still, these results do suggest that, on the most generous estimate, the numbers paying any attention to foreign affairs cannot at any time be much more than half the voting public. And the numbers genuinely concerned about any given foreign policy issue can seldom exceed a fraction of this half, especially since the most politically alert citizens most often interest themselves in domestic problems or local or state affairs. Surveys of differing samples of the population suggest a maximum proportion of around 16 or 17 per cent really caring about foreign policy.[7]

In makeup the foreign policy public represents the total population even less than does the voting public. Among those from whom pollsters can extract expressions of opinion on foreign policy the proportion of professional men and businessmen runs very high; that of clerical and skilled workers less high; that of unskilled workers and farmers markedly low. Proportions also vary with education. Among white collar workers those with only a grammar school education profess no opinion twice as often as high school graduates and three times as often as college graduates.[8] Even more than the voting public, the foreign policy public gives undue representation to those who are

[7] V. O. Key, Jr., *Public Opinion and American Democracy* (New York, 1961), pp. 173–174; Alfred O. Hero, Jr., *Americans in World Affairs* (Boston, 1959), *Mass Media and World Affairs* (Boston, 1959), and *Opinion Leaders in American Communities* (Boston, 1959).

[8] Key, *Public Opinion*, pp. 332–334.

wealthier and better educated. The only counterweight comes from people active in politics and not wholly absorbed by domestic affairs. Since the foreign policy public is so small, these people form a significant force within it, and other survey data show them most likely to be men or women energetically on the climb from low- or middle-level treads on the economic-social stairway.[9]

Oddly, considering their educational level, citizens interested in foreign policy tend to take unqualified stands and hold opinions dogmatically. A graph of poll results on a domestic issue is apt to look like a camel's hump or like two capital J's back to back, showing some opinion at the extremes, but most clustering around midway positions. A comparable graph for a foreign policy issue will resemble a single capital J or at most a capital U. No doubt this difference results in part from the fact that citizens feel impelled to reach compromises with one another. On an economic issue one man may favor capital and another labor, but each wants a solution with which the other can live. Apparently with the interests in question those of all Americans as against those of people in some foreign country, the citizen sees less reason to seek middle ground. Also, foreign policy debates often involve remote and unfamiliar things, and even informed and interested people may comprehend the issues by association or analogy. A Michigan Survey Research Center poll on relations with the U.S.S.R. found one interviewee thinking in the language of the boxing

[9] Robert A. Dahl, *Who Governs? Democracy and Power in an American City* (New Haven, 1961), pp. 282–301.

23

ring, another seeing parallels with relationships among his neighbors, and still another relying on parables from the Bible.[10] Today's foreign policy public can be characterized as not only overweighted with the prosperous, well educated, and politically active but also as opinionated and unpredictable.

If the foreign policy public of the late nineteenth century resembled today's, it numbered between 1.5 and 3 million, or something between 10 and 20 per cent of the voting public. The fact that many fewer Americans had high school or college diplomas would argue for the lower figure; the fact that many more had strong old-country ties, for the higher. Whatever the case, the majority would have come from the 500,000 or so who had graduated from colleges and the 1 to 1.5 million who had graduated from high school. Because interest in foreign affairs has to be fed by a constant flow of information from other parts of the globe, a high proportion would also have been concentrated in urban areas where daily newspapers circulated. The foreign policy public would thus have contained fewer farmers and rural dwellers than the voting public as a whole. The proportion of men or women active in politics would have been high. When we speak of public opinion about colonies in the 1890s, we mean, probably, opinion circulating within a comparatively well-to-do, well-educated, well-read, and politically active public, numbering less than 3 million and living mostly in cities.

How did politicians sense opinion changes within this

[10] Key, *Public Opinion*, p. 258.

24

foreign policy public? They could not count on economic or social class interests to predetermine positions on specific issues. Knowing this public to include the educated and the politically active, they could foresee possible disagreement, especially since, in an era of fiercely competing dailies, city dwellers had many differing sources of information. If they calculated also that members of this public might arrive at extreme positions by unpredictable thought processes, how could politicians forecast what the foreign policy public would approve or disapprove?

Obviously no generalization can cover all cases. A certain number of well-entrenched representatives or senators with primarily rural constituencies could afford to be recklessly individualistic. John Tyler Morgan, a white-mustached former Confederate general and four-term senator from Alabama, would deliver a jingo oration whenever occasion arose. Judging from his surviving papers, he almost never received a letter of praise or condemnation from a constituent. The people who wrote to him about foreign policy were mostly citizens of other states.[11]

Only representatives and senators in conspicuous leadership posts had to commit themselves at early points in debate. As veteran politicians, they would often in the past have gauged public reactions. No matter how new the issue, it would not put them in the position of advertisers offering wholly untested products to the market. In fore-

[11] Morgan's papers are in the Library of Congress. An article based on them and supporting the point made here is August C. Radke's "Senator Morgan and the Nicaragua Canal," *Alabama Review*, XII (Jan. 1959), 5–34.

casting public reactions they probably depended more on inference from past experience than on any set of present indicators.

The large majority of politicians could afford to postpone a stand, waiting either until events forced them to speak or until signs showed clearly what would command approval among interested voters in their districts or states.

While most congressmen could delay because they lacked responsibility, Presidents and Secretaries of State could take their time because, paradoxically, they had so much responsibility. The idea of leadership by the executive branch had much less acceptance in the nineties than later. Cleveland and McKinley executed the will of the people as reflected in resolutions passed by Congress. On the Hawaiian issue of 1893 and the Philippine issue of 1898, each initially took the position that he should postpone decision until the public will became plain, and neither met much criticism for doing so.

What registered in Washington as effective opinion need not have been any set of immediate reactions from segments of the foreign policy public. On the contrary, politicians read varying signals received over several days, weeks, or even months. Members of Congress making immediate statements received echoes telling them something not only about the inclinations of the interested public but also about its size and intensities of feeling. Depending on these echoes, congressmen might clarify, expand, amend, or change what they had said at the outset. Others, including Presidents and Secretaries of State, could watch the behavior of this vanguard while keeping their own ears open.

To reconstruct an individual performance is difficult. Henry Cabot Lodge is an example. A member of the House from 1887 to 1893 and a senator after 1893, Lodge not only served on the Foreign Relations Committee but also wrote magazine articles and made frequent speeches about foreign affairs. He had to take a stand on any new issue affecting American relations with other states; the *Congressional Record* and the daily press recorded what he said. His manuscripts in the Massachusetts Historical Society reveal the reactions he received by mail and tell something about people he saw and impressions he obtained through conversation. Nevertheless these sources, though ample, do not say what Lodge looked for or listened for.

We cannot know with certainty how Lodge estimated the criticism or approval of a constituent. How would he assay whether a critic took an issue seriously enough to let it determine his vote at the next election? How would he judge whether or not a determined critic had potential for swaying others, including others who did not necessarily care about the specific issue? Would someone who applauded the senator's initial statement feel betrayed if, in response to criticism, Lodge changed his stand? If so, would the aggrieved man influence others? Only in a lifetime among Lodge's papers and other Massachusetts political records could one reconstruct the elements entering into such calculations.

To generalize from partial data about how numbers of politicians judged opinion requires guesswork. Further borrowing from social science, may, however, permit what V. O. Key calls "tutored conjecture," for political sociologists have studied the breeding of public opinion and noted how often people rely on other people to tell them what they should think about a given public issue.

In his classic *American Commonwealth*, first published in 1888, James Bryce wrote of England having "three sets of persons . . . Those who make opinion, those who receive and hold opinion, those who have no opinion at all." As to whether the United States had a group of opinion makers, he said:

> There are individual men corresponding to individuals in that English set, and probably quite as numerous. There are journalists of great ability, there are a few literary men, clergymen and teachers, a good many lawyers, some business men, some few politicians. But they are isolated and unorganized, and do not constitute a class. . . . In England the profession of opinion-making and leading is the work of specialists; in America . . . of amateurs. . . . in America opinion does not originate in a particular class, but grows up in the nation at large, though, of course, there are leading minds in the nation who have more to do with its formation than the run of their fellow citizens.[12]

The agrarian novelist Hamlin Garland wrote in the early nineties of opinion in Midwestern small towns being shaped

[12] James Bryce, *The American Commonwealth*, 3rd ed., 2 vols. (New York, 1894), II, 317–324.

by preachers, soldiers, and politicians.[13] In the following decade the pioneer sociologist Edward A. Ross declared categorically:

> Every editor, politician, banker, capitalist, railroad president, employer, clergyman, or judge has a following with whom his opinion has weight. He, in turn, is likely to have *his* authorities. The anatomy of collective opinion shows it to be organized from centers and subcenters, forming a kind of intellectual feudal system.[14]

In detailed studies of Muncie, Indiana, in the 1920s and 1930s, Robert and Helen Lynd described leadership of opinion and virtual control over municipal affairs as vested in a small elite of wealthy families. Subsequent community studies lent support to the Lynds' findings. In time, C. Wright Mills and others were to hypothesize a nationwide "power elite." [15]

The work culminating in Mills's hypothesis centered more on power than on opinion. Another stream of research, led by Paul Lazarsfeld, ran in a different direction. Focusing first on how individual voters made candidate choices, this research uncovered influences that had little or no connection with power relationships. Voters were found to seek information and advice from acquaintances whose

---

[13] Hamlin Garland, *A Spoil of Office* (Boston, 1892), p. 265.

[14] Edward A. Ross, *Social Psychology* (New York, 1908), p. 248.

[15] Robert S. and Helen M. Lynd, *Middletown* (New York, 1929) and *Middletown in Transition* (New York, 1937); W. Lloyd Warner and Paul S. Lunt, *The Social Life of a Modern Community* (New Haven, 1941); Floyd Hunter, *Community Power Structure* (Chapel Hill, 1953); C. Wright Mills, *The Power Elite* (New York, 1956).

judgment they respected. The personal influence of these individuals often outweighed the influence of newspapers, magazines, or other media. Instead of garnering firsthand impressions, many relied on others to sift these media for them.[16]

Individuals exercising such influence did not form an easily identifiable group. Studying a small town not far from New York, Robert K. Merton found that on local issues townspeople looked for guidance to men whose business and other interests lay primarily within the community. On national and international issues they looked instead to citizens with interests and activities not centered solely in the town whose reading included metropolitan dailies and national magazines.[17]

With Elihu Katz, Lazarsfeld conducted a survey among women in Decatur, Illinois. They found that the women did not seek advice from any one group or type. Depending on the questions in their minds, they accepted guidance from those among their acquaintance who seemed to have the most experience or information. For advice on which brands to buy in the grocery store they looked to mothers of large families; on clothing styles or movies, to girls of

[16] Paul F. Lazarsfeld, Bernard Berelson, and Hazel Gaudet, *The People's Choice* (New York, 1944), deals with Erie County, Pa., during the presidential campaign of 1940. Further analysis was made of Elmira, N. Y., during the 1948 election in Bernard Berelson, Paul F. Lazarsfeld, and William McPhee, *Voting* (Chicago, 1954).

[17] Robert K. Merton, "Patterns of Influence: A Study of Interpersonal Influence and Communications Behavior in a Local Community," in Paul F. Lazarsfeld and Frank Stanton, eds., *Communications Research, 1948–49* (New York, 1949), pp. 180–219.

fifteen to twenty-four; on candidates and political issues, to well-educated, unmarried, gregarious young women. The latter in turn obtained advice from male friends with experience or special knowledge of politics. Lazarsfeld and Katz write:

> For leadership in political discussion people mainly turn to others like themselves. The banker and mayor and union officer may be "opinion leaders" in a distant sense, but ordinary voters listen to near-by influencers. For this reason, one might properly speak less of leaders than of a complex web of opinion-leading relationships. It is true that one can single out those individuals who are more likely than others to be at the center of several such relationships and call them "opinion leaders." . . . But when it is found also that the people so singled out as leaders report, in turn, that they *seek advice* on politics more than others . . . we are reminded again that in practice there must be unending circuits of leadership relationships running through the community, like a nerve system through the body.[18]

The most recent studies of American communities have found relationships of equal complexity determining not only opinions but also decisions and hence the exercise of

[18] Elihu Katz and Paul F. Lazarsfeld, *Personal Influence: The Part Played by People in the Flow of Mass Communications* (Glencoe, Ill., 1955), p. 325.

31

power. Robert Dahl discovered New Haven to have not just one elite but different leadership groups for practically every class of public issue. Others report similar findings.[19]

Social scientists' studies suggest one way of arriving at "tutored conjecture" about opinion movements within the small public that would have been interested in the colonial issue. It is to look for individuals who probably led opinion on this issue. Assuming that politicians would have known who these individuals were and would have paid special attention to their views and reactions, one might thus obtain some idea of how effective opinion came into being. Such studies as those of Lazarsfeld and Dahl warn, however, against looking solely for local elites, for people with influence or power in one realm do not necessarily act as guides or bellwethers in others.

Studies identifying leadership types in the present-day foreign policy public aid the search for Americans who might have led opinion on colonial expansion in the nineties. One such study describes the handful of men from whom folk in a Midwestern suburb sought advice about American interests, policies, and activities abroad. Characteristically, these men were "highly educated, wealthy, Protestant, Anglo-Saxon," and well into middle age. They owed their influence, says the study, to interest in foreign affairs combined with "high standing in the legal profession, or a high executive position in industry, banking, or commerce,"

---

[19] Dahl, *Who Governs?* See particularly Aaron Wildavsky, *Leadership in a Small Town* (Totowa, N. J., 1964), and Nelson Polsby, *Community Power and Political Theory* (New Haven, 1963).

some experience in Washington or with an American overseas mission, frequent travel abroad, wide reading, often in foreign periodicals, and personal acquaintance with movers and shakers in the worlds of journalism and politics.[20]

Not in the habit of pressing their opinions on others, such men do not write letters to the newspapers or seek opportunities to make speeches. Reporters may solicit statements by them, and organizations may invite them to speak. Most often, however, their views get into circulation because individuals (called "talkers" in another sociological study[21]) come to them for advice and then quote their views to others in the interested public.

Another, larger-scale study by James N. Rosenau reports similar findings.[22] It deals with a thousand-odd men and women invited to Washington in 1958 to discuss means of influencing public attitudes toward foreign aid. Chosen by the President and State Department with aid from the U.S. Chamber of Commerce and other such bodies, they formed what Rosenau regards as a representative sample of an interlaced nationwide leadership group. Like leaders of foreign policy opinion in the Midwestern suburb, these men and

[20] Kenneth P. Adler and Davis Bobrow, "Interest and Influence in Foreign Affairs," *Public Opinion Quarterly*, XX (Spring 1956), 89–101.

[21] Robert E. Agger and Vincent Ostrom, "The Political Structure of a Small Community," *ibid.*, pp. 81–89.

[22] James N. Rosenau, *National Leadership and Foreign Policy: A Case Study in the Mobilization of Public Support* (Princeton, N. J., 1963). See also Bernard C. Cohen, *The Political Process and Foreign Policy: The Making of the Japanese Peace Settlement* (Princeton, N. J., 1957), pp. 101–103.

women were successful, well-to-do, high in social status, well connected, relatively well educated, up on current affairs, and widely traveled.

Rosenau also notes three other characteristics not evident in the smaller sampling. First, participants in the conference not only passed opinions down some ladder of influence but exchanged ideas and influenced one another. Second, they had, as a rule, some means of communicating with people whom they did not personally know, either by appearing on radio or television panels or making public speeches or, in some cases, writing books or articles. Third, they divided into two classifications: the "continental," with nationwide perspective and actual or potential influence in groups not distinguishable by interest or location; and the "segmented," with essentially local, regional or organizational perspectives and influence primarily within localities, industries, unions, or professions. Those in the "continental" group tended to be more in harmony with and more influential with the executive branch; those in the "segmented" group, closer to and more effective with members of Congress.

Much remains to be learned about present-day foreign policy leadership. The studies just cited do little more than sketch hypotheses which later research will have to test and either amplify or modify. Nevertheless a historian can use these hypotheses without simply accepting them unquestioningly, for they appeal to common sense. Faced with complex questions, citizens are likely to turn for guidance to those who profess knowledge. These men will turn to

34

others whom they think specially qualified, and so on and on until the questions reach those who know others as well equipped as they but none better equipped.

While the same process might take place regardless of the issue, it would not always involve the same individuals. On a local school bond issue the leaders of opinion might be municipal officials, bankers, real estate dealers, or educators. On a matter of labor legislation they might be union officers, plant managers, or lawyers. With the issue one of foreign policy, the interested public would probably seek guidance from men with the characteristics that survey data indicate: reputations for good judgment, as proven by success in business or a profession; some special knowledge of the world, obtained by some combination of travel and reading; and given the seeming arcaneness of foreign policy and diplomacy, probably also some firsthand acquaintance with the ways of Washington and perhaps of other capitals.

Assuming that foreign policy opinion leaders existed in the late nineteenth century, how can one identify them? Obviously not with polls or questionnaires or other contemporary devices. What we must use instead are biographies and biographical registers, such as *Who's Who in America*, indicating which men combined such qualifications as business or professional success, special knowledge of the outside world, and acquaintance with American or foreign statesmen. Second, we can use the press to see whether local reporters went to these individuals for interviews or statements, and, if so, whether they were approached as people whose names would be known to all or whether they needed identifying tags. We can also look afield to see who was quoted or mentioned in papers outside his home town.

Two objections may be raised against such use of the press. Some political scientists and sociologists have protested the survey technique of asking people to name others whom they think powerful or influential, pointing out that respondents are apt to name their best publicized or most conspicuously wealthy fellow citizens. The results then create a portrait of a tiny power elite and obscure the many leadership groups called into being by differing circumstances and issues.[23] Using newspapers, one similarly obtains only the names of the very prominent and thus runs equal risk of coming up with wrong results.

The second objection arises because of the daily newspaper's large, mixed audience. Its editors may give space to an individual solely because of his celebrity and potential interest to numbers of readers. The individual's views need not carry weight with the small public specially interested in the issue he addressed. Leafing through a major daily in

[23] See Peter H. Rossi, "Power and Community Structure," *Midwest Journal of Political Science*, IV (Nov. 1960), 390–401; Raymond E. Wolfinger, "A Plea for a Decent Burial," *American Sociological Review*, XXVII (Dec. 1962), 841–847; Polsby, *Community Power and Political Theory, passim;* Wildavsky, *Leadership in a Small Town*, pp. 303–304; John Walton, "Substance and Artifact: The Current Status of Research on Community Power Structure," *American Journal of Sociology*, LXXI (Jan. 1966), 430–438; William A. Gamson, "Reputation and Resources in Community Politics," *ibid.*, LXXII (Sept. 1966), 121–131; and John Walton, "Discipline, Method, and Community Power: A Note on the Sociology of Knowledge," *American Sociological Review*, XXXI (Oct. 1966), 684–689.

the mid-1960s one would find it hard to extract names of genuine leaders of opinion on foreign policy. Even *The New York Times* and the *Wall Street Journal* refer infrequently to Robert A. Lovett, John McCloy, John Mc-Cone, McGeorge Bundy, and others who reputedly make up the contemporary foreign policy establishment. Why should dailies of the 1890s have done better?

Without fully meeting either objection, one can make a few points in defense. First, American cities of the late nineteenth century had small-town qualities that they have since lost. Herbert W. Bowen wrote of New York, the nation's biggest city, that it "was a snug and smug town in the eighteen-eighties, and it was possible to know everyone of importance there, at least by sight." Of Washington, D.C., with 150,000 inhabitants in 1890, it was said that "an old resident knew by sight everyone who kept a carriage." [24]

In the second place, the press of the period differed from today's. Wire services provided less copy, especially on international affairs. To flesh out stories, reporters and editors had to make more use of interviews with local citizens. With circulation of most dailies below a hundred thousand, even in the biggest cities, reporters and editors served relatively small reading communities, and, in consequence, could more easily single out recognizable opinion leaders.

Third, the press itself served as a medium of opinion guidance. While editorial writers probably molded opinion no more than they do today, news columns and editorial

[24] Herbert W. Bowen, *Recollections, Diplomatic and Undiplomatic* (New York, 1926), p. 95; Stephen Gwynn, ed., *The Letters and Friendships of Sir Cecil Spring Rice: A Record,* 2 vols. (London, 1929), I, 52.

pages portrayed drifts of opinion within a community. Bryce depicts the process. In *The American Common-wealth* he describes a businessman reading in a morning paper of Bismarck's announcement that Germany would enact protective tariffs. The news has some effect on him, which an editorial may intensify or weaken. On the commuter train he discusses the news with others. At his office he talks it over with still others and perhaps looks at comment in other newspapers. By afternoon, says Bryce, "his mind is beginning to settle down into a definite view." Bryce continues:

> Meanwhile, a similar process has been going on in the minds of others, and particularly of the journalists, whose business it is to discover what people are thinking. The evening paper has collected the opinions of morning papers, and is rather more positive in its forecast of results. Next day the leading journals have articles still more definite and positive in approval or condemnation and in prediction of consequences to follow; and the opinion of ordinary minds, hitherto fluid and undetermined, has begun to crystallize into a solid mass. This is the second stage. Then debate and controversy begin. The men and the newspapers who approve . . . argue with those who do not; they find out who are friends and who opponents.[25]

[25] Bryce, *American Commonwealth*, II, 248.

38

In other words, editorials served as expressions of opinion developing within and circulating out from leadership groups. Occasionally they reflected idiosyncrasies of editors or publishers. Individual editors, as Bryce observed, belonged to the primary set of opinion-formers. Even so, he noted, "A journalist . . . is obliged to hark back if he has inadvertently taken up a position disagreeable to his *clientèle*, because the proprietors of the paper have their circulation to consider." In general, probably, daily newspapers played roles as "talkers."

None of these three points is conclusive. Even in small communities reputational surveys yield distorted results. The press may have singled out for quotation or mention only the most well-known men and not those whose counsel others actually sought. Reporters' judgments as to those worth interviewing need not have coincided with judgments among the bulk of the interested public. Even if the press indicated trends in opinion, it did not necessarily indicate the sources of those trends. Newspapermen may have been "talkers" talking to "talkers."

A fourth point to be made, however, is that there simply exist no other sources. Lacking any other data except from biographies and papers of prominent men and the daily press, one has to hope that the sampling of opinion leaders discoverable in the press somehow represents the larger and more varied leadership group whose members played their parts and passed away. Without such an assumption one could not approach the questions raised in the preceding chapter.

39

But we look for relationships as intricate and delicate as those among layered cobwebs. Politicians, we assume, recognized the likely opinion leaders on such an issue as colonial expansion. We assume further that they watched these individuals for indications of the directions in which opinion was likely to move. Each politician would, however, have had some means of double-checking. Lodge, for example, had a son-in-law in Boston who questioned railroad conductors about conversations among commuters.[26] In addition, each politician had methods of influencing opinion. During the crisis with Spain in April 1898 Secretary of State William R. Day pressed his newspaper friends to write about antiwar feeling among businessmen, while warhawks in the Senate urged reporter friends to play up contrary evidence.[27] At times politicians called signals for the public.

Opinion leaders not in office and the larger interested public had a similar two-way relationship. The prominent, well-read, well-traveled, and well-connected citizen might, in a first reaction, commit himself to a stand. Sensing later that for some reason his peers or public would not endorse this stand, he might back down or shift ground. Many businessmen, clergymen, and editors who opposed war with Spain early in 1898 changed front when they saw, or thought they saw, the multitudes turning jingo. Even when one

[26] A. P. Gardner to Lodge, April 5, 1898, Private Papers of Henry Cabot Lodge, Massachusetts Historical Society.

[27] L. A. Coolidge to Lodge, July 27, 1898, *ibid.;* William E. Chandler to Paul Dana, April 7, April 13, 1898, Private Papers of William E. Chandler, Library of Congress.

40

identifies men who probably served as leaders within the foreign policy public, he has to remember that, no less than holders of office, they were influenced by as well as influential with their constituencies.

One has to remember further the open-endedness of each network of relations between politicians, local opinion leaders, and an interested public. Prior to Dewey's victory at Manila few Americans articulated opinions about colonial expansion. By the time of the President's decision to annex the islands most of the three million or so in the potential foreign policy public were doing so or had done so. And this suddenly enlarged public need not have had the same characteristics as the smaller public originally interested. Indeed, it may have differed in both composition and leadership.

Finally, one has to keep in mind the fact that no network had a fixed character or an existence entirely independent of others. Politicians paid attention to many different publics, listening not only for pitch notes from each but for harmonies, discords, and relative volumes. Nonoffice-holding opinion leaders belonged to many publics and perhaps led in more than one. Citizens serving as talkers within the foreign policy public may have performed the same function in other publics or, for that matter, been leaders in one and talkers in others. Even within the foreign policy public, roles may have changed. A man leading opinion on tariff or trade issues could have turned talker when the issue had to do with strategic requirements. The foreign policy public consists of many publics, each made up of men and women with other interests.

Normally the party system would bring together the many specialized publics, leading voters who neither know nor care about a particular policy area to accept the position of an interested minority as right and wise because it becomes associated with their positions on subjects about which they do know and care. Public opinion on a partisan issue differs from public opinion on an issue not yet a party matter.[28] But the foreign policy public does not always enter such consortiums. The interest groups that bargain within parties sometimes find it hard to define what they want and need abroad. The farm bloc of the 1890s, for example, knew it wanted lower freight rates at home but felt doubt as to whether overseas colonies would do good by permitting more export trade or do harm by providing cheap-labor competition. Moreover, when dealing with foreign policy issues, framers of party doctrine feel more obligation to be patriotic, couching stands in terms of the nation's interests rather than those of special groups.

In any case, we can here study the formation of public attitudes without having to take account until a late point of the intricate calculation and bargaining that transformed these attitudes into the positions of mass political parties.

[28] Though this point was suggested in Berelson, Lazarsfeld, and Mc-Phee, *Voting*, pp. 137–149, its chief development is in two works that, in part, take issue with the Lazarsfeld studies: Angus Campbell, Gerald Gurin, and Warren E. Miller, *The Voter Decides* (Evanston, 1954), and Angus Campbell *et al.*, *The American Voter* (New York, 1960). See also George Belknap and Angus Campbell, "Political Party Identification and Attitudes Toward Foreign Policy," *Public Opinion Quarterly*, XV (Winter 1951–52), 601–623, and Key, *Public Opinion*, pp. 458–466.

Using criteria supplied by recent survey research and drawing on such fragments as we have from the era, we can try to identify a few of the probable leaders of opinion. After doing so we can go on to consider the influences that may have shaped their stands.

III

THE ESTABLISHMENT: BOSTON AND NEW YORK

Owing to historic factors, the pretensions of its old families, and an essentially mercantile economy, Boston and its suburbs had many residents equipped by education, attainments, and connections to lead opinion on the colonial issue.

Thomas Jefferson Coolidge typified this comparatively large foreign policy elite. His autobiography and collected private papers tell us a good deal about him, and from recent historical studies by Barbara Solomon, Arthur Mann, and Geoffrey Blodgett we know that he had little to do with molding public opinion on domestic issues.[1] He thus

---

[1] Barbara Solomon, *Ancestors and Immigrants* (Cambridge, Mass., 1956), Arthur Mann, *Yankee Reformers in the Urban Age* (Cambridge, Mass., 1954), and Geoffrey Blodgett, *The Gentle Reformers: Massachusetts Democrats in the Cleveland Era* (Cambridge, Mass., 1966). Basic information on Coolidge is taken from Thomas Jefferson Coolidge, *Auto-*

exemplifies the specialized opinion leader—a prototype member of what today we call the foreign policy establishment.

Born in 1831 into a securely rich family, Coolidge took his primary and secondary schooling in England and Switzerland and then attended Harvard. Entering business, he became, by his late forties, president of the Merchants Bank of Boston and a heavy investor in railroads, serving at one time as president of the Santa Fe and, at another, as a director of the Chicago, Burlington, and Quincy. Owning land in the center of Birmingham, Alabama, he built stores that prospered from Birmingham's sudden boom. Not all his gambles succeeded. An electric-light plant in Topeka, Kansas, for example, resulted in a loss. Its optimistic manager wrote, "A coupon cutter and a Dividend payer, are the next inventions I look for in connection with this versatile agent"; but he proved unable to deliver.[2] Nevertheless, in association with other financiers, Coolidge made many a dollar from well-timed purchases and sales of bonds, stocks, lands, and buildings.

Owning most if not all the characteristics of a robber baron, Coolidge could write the following record of a conversation with a rental agent: "He said the woman who occupies the Anderson property cannot pay rent. I directed him to turn her out and I would make the house into two tenements which could be rented." On another occasion

biography (Boston, 1902) and Allen Johnson and Dumas Malone, eds., *Dictionary of American Biography*, 20 vols. and two supplementary vols. (New York, 1928–58)—hereafter cited as *DAB*—IV, 395.

[2] E. Wilder to Coolidge, May 24, 1887, Private Papers of Thomas Jefferson Coolidge, Massachusetts Historical Society.

45

Coolidge advised a friend not to accept a certain mortgage, cautioning, "It is very hard to collect either interest or capital from the Church without putting your hand in your pocket to help the good cause." Property in Birmingham attracted him because of "the endless supply of black labor." When profit beckoned he speculated in any commodity, including opium.[3]

In domestic politics Coolidge also showed the temper of a robber baron. One of his letters gave marching orders for the senators and representatives from Nebraska who "are obeying the C.B.&Q." As the largest shareholder in the Amoskeag Cotton Mills, he maintained an agent in Manchester, New Hampshire, who labored to prevent "radical legislation." He himself spent time in Washington lobbying for protective duties on textiles.[4]

Yet the press quoted him, and politicians sought his views and estimates of public feeling only on foreign policy problems, and not even on cotton tariffs. Reporters for Boston papers and for the Springfield *Republican* sought him out during a crisis with Chile of 1891–92, a crisis with Britain four years later over the Venezuela-Guiana boundary, the blowing up of the *Maine*, war with Spain, and the question of whether or not to annex the Philippines. James G. Blaine, when Secretary of State for Benjamin Harrison, expressed interest in Coolidge's views on possible complications with Germany in the Pacific. Both of Massachusetts'

[3] Coolidge to A. D. Paton, Oct. 11, 1888; to John Codman, June 3, 1889; to W. H. Edwards, Dec. 8, 1887; to Dabney, Simmons, and Co., April 19, 1887, *ibid*.
[4] Coolidge to C. E. Perkins, April 18, 1888; H. F. Straw to Coolidge, Nov. 6, 1886; Coolidge to P. M. Moon, April 4, 1890, *ibid*.

senators solicited his reactions to their positions on other foreign policy issues, including colonial expansion.[5] Journalists in his home community and politicians in Washington evidently attached special weight to Coolidge's views on foreign policy.

He possessed unusually wide knowledge of the world. Fluent in French and familiar with English and European culture from his early education, he subsequently traveled much, not only in Europe but also in out-of-the-way places, such as Alexandria and Port au Prince, which most Americans discovered only as datelines on crisis reports. In 1889 he served as a delegate to the first Pan American Conference. In 1892–93 he spent a year as United States Minister to France.

Partly as a result of his travels and his diplomatic experience, Coolidge knew leading figures abroad. He could speak familiarly of such English and French statesmen as Joseph Chamberlain, Arthur Balfour, Jules Ferry, and Gabriel Hanotaux. He could name for President Harrison the men in England who would hold the keys to an international agreement on bimetallism and advise Massachusetts' Senator George F. Hoar on whether a proposed emissary would have the proper entree to this group.[6] Interested cit-

[5] Boston *Journal*, Jan. 3, 1892, Dec. 22, 1895, April 3, May 17, 1898; Boston *Herald*, Dec. 23, 1895, June 3, 1898; Boston *Globe*, Dec. 20, 1895, June 1, 1898; Springfield *Republican*, May 15, 1898; James G. Blaine to Hoar, April 25, 1892, Private Papers of George F. Hoar, Massachusetts Historical Society; Hoar to Coolidge, July 1, 1898, *ibid.;* Henry Cabot Lodge to Coolidge: Dec. 21, 1895, Sept. 6, 1898, Coolidge Papers; Aug. 11, 1898, Lodge Papers.

[6] Coolidge to Benjamin Harrison, June 29, 1891; to Hoar, July 11, 1891, Coolidge Papers.

izens and politicians probably looked to Coolidge as an opinion leader primarily because of his firsthand knowledge of foreign places and inside knowledge of foreign politics.

Coolidge's near contemporary, William C. Endicott, possessed comparable qualifications. A noted lawyer, onetime judge and holder of large and profitable railroad investments, he had been Secretary of War during Cleveland's first administration, and his daughter had married the celebrated English politician, Joseph Chamberlain. When in England, he met the great and near great, and through his daughter and her friends received inside news of British and European political developments. Like Coolidge, Endicott could set Washington straight as to who pulled strings in London, and both politicians and newspapermen looked upon him as an authority on foreign affairs.[7]

Richard Olney did not have quite the background of Coolidge or Endicott.[8] Though of an old family, he came from western Massachusetts, and he had a bachelor's degree from Brown rather than Harvard. A hardworking, somewhat solitary railroad lawyer, he traveled little and gained none of Coolidge's or Endicott's firsthand knowledge of foreign statesmen. Before the 1890s he could have qualified as a leader of opinion on certain domestic issues, but hardly on foreign policy. In Cleveland's second administration, how-

[7] The only biographical sketch of Endicott is in *DAB*, VI, 158–159. A collection of family correspondence, including a few letters from Mary Endicott Chamberlain, is in the Massachusetts Historical Society. A few other letters are among the Private Papers of Joseph Chamberlain, Birmingham University Library, Birmingham, England.

[8] See Henry James, *Richard Olney and His Public Service* (Boston, 1923), and the Private Papers of Richard Olney, Library of Congress.

ever, Olney served first as Attorney General and then, for two years, as Secretary of State. Coupled with his professional distinction, this experience caused him too to become a target of reporters' questions and of inquiring letters from politicians.

The circle of foreign policy leaders in Boston probably included also President Charles W. Eliot of Harvard.[9] Of a high-caste family and equipped, of course, with a Harvard diploma, Eliot had lived in France and Germany and made many trips to England. He could claim friendship with Bryce and other eminent Englishmen, and he could speak with authority not only on European education but also on English government and the English colonial system.

Perhaps the circle also included Eliot's counterpart at Tufts College, Elmer H. Capen. Not a Brahmin, Capen had grown up in modest circumstances and received his education at Tufts. After success as a Universalist minister he returned to Tufts as both president and head of the department of political science. So far as can be discovered, such knowledge as he had of foreign affairs came from reading rather than travel or acquaintance with foreign leaders. Yet Boston newspapers sought and quoted his views on Hawaii and the Philippines, and John D. Long, a former governor and McKinley's Secretary of the Navy, wrote of Capen later:

> He was a constant attendant at the Massachusetts Club . . . and no member of that club, although

[9] Henry James, *Charles W. Eliot*, 2 vols. (Boston, 1930).

49

made up as it was of men distinguished in political life, had a keener interest in affairs of state, in affairs that concerned the welfare of his country, in great political and economic questions . . . and no man spoke upon them with more thoroughness of appreciation or better information.[10]

Similar evidence exists for Samuel J. Elder, a Rhode Islander, a Yale alumnus, and Boston's foremost courtroom lawyer, to whose forcefulness and persuasiveness William Howard Taft later bore witness. In the late eighties and early nineties Elder led a successful battle for an international copyright convention, coming in touch with writers, publishers, and politicians who championed the cause in England. Though we know few details of his movements, a memoir by his daughter mentions "many ocean journeys to Europe or the tropic seas." In any case Elder was, along with Coolidge, Endicott, and Olney, among the first men to whom Boston newspapermen turned for statements about foreign policy issues.[11]

Reporters may have sought Elder's views partly because of his reputed popularity and influence with Boston's large Irish population. Though a Yankee and a Protestant, Elder represented Irish-American politicians in court cases and sometimes drew invitations to speak at Irish meetings. In the

[10] Universalist Club of Boston, *Elmer Hewitt Capen* (Boston, n.d. [1905?]), p. 18. See also *DAB*, III, 481.

[11] Margaret M. Elder *et al.*, *The Life of Samuel J. Elder* (New Haven, 1925). The reference to his travels appears on p. 337. Taft's tribute is the Foreword to the volume. See also *DAB*, VI, 66–67.

Irish Catholic Boston *Pilot*, his words on the colonial issue received more attention than those of any other local Yankee except Lodge.[12]

Irish-Americans had foreign policy leaders of their own, among them Patrick A. Collins and Thomas J. Gargan. Coming to the United States as a child, Collins had educated himself and then won admission to and graduated from the Harvard Law School. Though only moderately successful at the bar, he made a mark in politics. After a term in the state legislature he went to Congress and then, from 1895 to 1897, served as Cleveland's Consul General in London. A member of the Land League and a founder of the Irish National League, he made himself heard on the Irish question more than on any other topic, but the *Pilot* quoted his comments on many foreign policy issues, including colonial expansion.[13]

Also a self-educated lawyer, Gargan had been active in politics, served on a number of appointive commissions, and in addition, held office as director of a bank and an insurance company. Much traveled, he exhibited a wide range of foreign policy interests, speaking with special authority about Latin America, where he had spent the longest time. After soliciting Protestant Yankee backing for a protest against the Italian government's seizure of papal property, he made repayment by joining an essentially Protestant

[12] Elder *et al.*, *Elder*, pp. 194–195; Boston *Globe*, May 8, 1898; Boston *Pilot*, May 6, 12, 15, and 30, 1898.
[13] Michael Philip Curran, *Life of Patrick A. Collins, with Some of His Most Notable Public Addresses* (Norwood, Mass., 1906). See, for example, Boston *Pilot*, May 10, 1898.

51

campaign to aid Armenians persecuted by Turks. Business success and a reputation for honesty, together with participation in the Armenian crusade, gave Gargan standing with Yankees as well as Irish-Americans, and not only the *Pilot* but also the Boston *Evening Transcript* and the Springfield *Republican* noted his comments on the Hawaiian and Philippine issues.[14]

Given the climate of the 1890s, the circle of foreign policy opinion leaders in Boston probably included some clergymen. Their pulpits guaranteed them access to a public, and Monday-morning newspapers customarily enlarged that public by reporting and quoting from sermons delivered the day before. Among those who preached on foreign policy issues and whose words may have carried weight were Minot J. Savage and Thomas Van Ness, both Unitarians, both widely traveled, and both authors of successful books, Savage's on the implications of Darwinism for religion and Van Ness's on, among other things, militarism and pacifism.[15]

Conceivably, a list of opinion leaders should contain in addition some writers and publicists. Obvious possibilities include John Fiske, author of the essay "Manifest Destiny"

[14] *Thomas J. Gargan, A Memorial* (Boston, 1910); Boston *Evening Transcript*, May 9, 1898; Springfield *Republican*, May 12, 1898.

[15] On Savage, see *DAB*, XVI, 389–390, and his own *Life Questions* (Boston, 1892), *The Irrepressible Conflict Between Two World Theories: Five Lectures Dealing with Christianity and Evolutionary Thought* (Boston, 1892), and *Religion for To-day* (Boston, 1897); on Van Ness, see *Who's Who in America, 1914–1915* (Chicago, 1914), p. 2405, and Van Ness, *The Coming Religion* (Boston, 1893) and *The Religion of New England* (Boston, 1926).

and other works which won acclaim in England as well as at home, Henry Adams' brilliant but dour brother, Brooks, and Francis H. Underwood, a founder of the *Atlantic Monthly* and at one time United States consul at Glasgow. In 1893 the Boston *Globe* asked both Adams and Underwood for statements on the Hawaiian issue. In view of Adams' reputation as an eccentric and Underwood's reported penchant for letting the world know that he had never received just recognition, there seems some question as to how far their influence would have run.[16]

At a fairly early point one feels oneself among "talkers." A reporter for the Boston *Herald* sought a comment on the Philippine issue from James J. Myers, a Harvard graduate, a corporation lawyer, a director of many companies, and a member of Boston's best clubs. Myers responded that "the soundest and best minds" had not yet come to an opinion. George Fox Tucker, a lawyer and writer who had published, among other things, a study of the Monroe Doctrine, answered a similar question by quoting Richard Olney. Edwin Ginn, a successful textbook publisher, told the *Globe,* "As far as I have been able to ascertain the opinion of prudent men is that we should hesitate long before adopting any line of action contrary to" precedent.[17] In

[16] Milton Berman, *John Fiske* (Cambridge, Mass., 1961); Arthur F. Beringause, *Brooks Adams, A Biography* (New York, 1955); *DAB*, XIX, 112–113; Bliss Perry, *Park-Street Papers* (Boston, 1908), pp. 203–277.

[17] For Myers, see Boston *Herald,* May 8, 1898; for Tucker and Ginn, Boston *Globe,* May 8, 1898. On Myers, see *Who's Who in America, 1914–1915,* p. 1705; on Tucker, see *ibid.,* p. 2377, and his own *A Quaker Home* (Boston, 1891); on Ginn, see *DAB*, VII, 317, *In Memory of Edwin Ginn, 1838–1914: Memorial Service at the South Congregational Church,*

Winchester, the suburb where he lived, Ginn may have been more assertive, for Samuel McCall, a onetime governor, recalled later that Ginn "was a man for whom the people of . . . Winchester had a great regard." [18] For the wider public reached by the metropolitan dailies, however, neither Ginn nor Tucker nor Myers stood forth as an opinion guide.

Researchers able to stage interviews in Boston of the 1890s would undoubtedly come up with more names of men who played genuine leadership roles, for trying to diagram the influence structure of a nineteenth-century community is like trying to rebuild a jigsaw puzzle with only a few of the pieces. Some Bostonians almost certainly looked to Coolidge, Endicott, and Olney for advice on the question of whether or not the United States should acquire colonies. Perhaps some looked also to Eliot and Capen, and some Boston Irishmen relied on Collins and Gargan. Whether Elder, Savage, and Van Ness had influence is less certain, and this group shades off into another, represented by Myers, Tucker, and Ginn, which deferred to and echoed opinions borrowed from others. We cannot now know how many other men occupied places in or on the fringes of Boston's foreign policy establishment.

Upon those whom we can identify, all the influences discussed in Chapter I operated. Men such as Coolidge, Endi-

---

Boston, Sunday, March 1, 1914 (n.p., n.d.), and Thomas Bonaventure Lawler, *Seventy Years of Textbook Publishing: A History of Ginn and Company, 1867–1937* (Boston, 1938).

[18] *In Memory of Edwin Ginn*, p. 12.

cott, and Eliot had a sense of the nation's complex traditions. Most had some acquaintance with Darwinian ideas as
applied to current problems, and two, Fiske and Savage,
were leading Social Darwinist writers. As capitalists or corporation lawyers, Coolidge, Endicott, Olney, and Elder
watched out not only for the interests of their own companies or clients but for the general welfare of American
business. And some at least participated in what Hofstadter
calls the "psychic crisis." In 1891, when workingmen and
agrarians had only begun to agitate, Coolidge prophesied
darkly, "communism will in time destroy not only the stock
capital, but the bonds which are . . . the accumulation of
labor." [19] The distinction between these men and others sensitive to tradition, imbued with Darwinism, concerned
about business, or irrationally anxious about the future, lay
chiefly in their having special familiarity with, even inside
knowledge of, European politics.

For New York one cannot as easily single out a typical
individual. Boston's establishment had a clublike character.
Coolidge did business with Endicott, employed Olney as a
lawyer, met Eliot twice a month at meetings of the Harvard
Corporation, and so on. Though Coolidge had been a Democrat until the late 1880s and Endicott and Olney both remained Democrats through Cleveland's administrations, the
state's two Republican senators consulted them rather than
others, assuming apparently that they could speak for the
city's foreign policy public better than could party-line Republicans. It was a small, closely knit public. Reporting to

[19] Coolidge to C. E. Perkins, March 4, 1891, Coolidge Papers.

55

Speaker Reed its unanimous disapproval of Cleveland's menacing demand that Britain arbitrate her boundary dispute with Venezuela, Coolidge could write, "At every bank meeting, at every dinner, in every club, you meet only one opinion." [20] Almost the only other foreign policy public in Boston was that which Coolidge acknowledged to be taking the opposite view, the politically active Irish-Americans for whom Gargan and Collins could speak.

New York, of course, possessed a larger number of opinion leaders. Four times the size of Boston, it had not only a strong Irish element but also a well-organized German community, and all in all, a much more complex political structure. Its elite groups, as compared with those of Boston, contained many fewer men who had inherited money and social standing. Of those who had made the climb on their own, many had, of necessity, involved themselves in politics as more than occasional wire-pullers or employers of lobbyists. They had bargained directly with ward leaders, aldermen, state legislators, congressmen, and other granters of favors and franchises and hence had become associated with party factions in their city and state. As a result it is difficult to find in New York individuals who, like Coolidge in Boston, functioned as opinion leaders only on foreign policy issues.

To be sure, this apparent difference may be an illusion, attributable to differences between the daily newspapers of the two cities. Boston had a variety of dailies: the *Transcript* for old Yankees; the *Journal* for rock-ribbed Repub-

[20] Coolidge to Thomas B. Reed, Dec. 24, 1895, *ibid.*

licans; the *Herald* for Republicans with more taste for the heterodox and the sensational; the *Globe* for nonpolitical middle-class families; the *Post* for Yankee and Irish Democrats; and the *Pilot* for Irish Catholics. But this menu did not compare with New York's, where each major daily reflected the personality of an idiosyncratic publisher or editor: the *Evening Post*, Edwin L. Godkin; the *Herald*, James Gordon Bennett; the *Sun*, Charles A. Dana; the *Tribune*, Whitelaw Reid; the *World*, after 1883, Joseph Pulitzer; the *Journal*, founded in 1895, William Randolph Hearst; and the *Times*, after 1896, Adolph Ochs. Maybe these papers portray a relatively unspecialized foreign policy establishment, because the editors publicized the views of their friends, regardless of whether the issue was domestic or foreign. Perhaps they portray a relatively variegated establishment, because the editors had diverse tastes. On the other hand, as in Boston, the men whom the press singled out possessed special qualifications for guiding opinion on foreign policy issues, and politicians in Washington wrote to them for advice and for bulletins on the temper of the city and state.

Seeking a few possibly representative individuals, we could choose a capitalist comparable to Coolidge or Endicott. We could not choose from among the titans, such as Pierpont Morgan or Jacob Schiff of Kuhn, Loeb and Company, or a partner in the Standard Oil trust; for these powerful men, despite their education, wide travel, and professional interest in foreign investment and trade, took no evident part in leading or speaking for public opinion.

57

Morgan gave no sign of even holding a view on colonial expansion; Schiff came to an opinion only belatedly and hesitantly, after listening perplexedly to debate among friends; and the Standard partners remained silent even about proposals, such as that for annexing the Danish West Indies, in which one of their number had a direct financial interest.[21] While New York's foreign policy establishment may not have been as discrete as Boston's, it was not identifiable with what a C. Wright Mills of the day would have labeled its "power elite."

The New York capitalists to whom reporters and politicians turned during foreign policy debates were such men as Andrew Carnegie, the Scottish-born steelmaker who kept a castle in his homeland, hobnobbed with most of the leaders in the House of Commons, and dabbled in English

[21] Frederick Lewis Allen, *The Great Pierpont Morgan* (New York, 1949), pp. 193–194; Herbert L. Satterlee, *J. Pierpont Morgan, An Intimate Portrait* (New York, 1939), pp. 382–384, 484; Cyrus Adler, *Jacob H. Schiff, His Life and Letters*, 2 vols. (New York, 1929), I, 10, II, 327–340; Allan Nevins, *John D. Rockefeller: The Heroic Age of American Enterprise*, 2 vols. (New York, 1940), II, 178–180. Rockefeller's brother William managed Standard's continually expanding export operations; John D. Archbold, who succeeded Rockefeller as head of the trust, took great interest in these operations. W. H. Libby traveled a great deal after 1886, arranging foreign contracts and acquisitions. Other important figures in the company, including James McDonald, C. F. Lufkin, and E. T. Bedford, each made at least one business trip to Europe during the 1890s. There is no evidence, however, that any of these individuals showed particular interest in foreign politics. See Nevins, *John D. Rockefeller*, II, 443–444, and Ralph M. and Muriel Hidy, *History of the Standard Oil Company (New Jersey): Pioneering in Big Business, 1882–1911* (New York, 1955), pp. 122–154, 233–268. On the interest of Standard partner H. H. Rogers in the purchase of the Danish West Indies, see 57 Cong., 1 sess., *House Report* No. 2749, and Tansill, *Purchase of the Danish West Indies*, pp. 215, 245–246, 249–254.

politics almost as much as in American; Chauncey M. Depew, president of the New York Central Railroad, master of the after-dinner speech, and a continual transatlantic traveler who could talk of dining with Gladstone and Chamberlain and of exchanging chaffing cablegrams with Lord Rosebery; and Henry Villard, railroad promoter, backer of political journals in both the United States and Germany, frequent visitor to his German homeland, friend of many European leaders, and sometime consultant on American affairs to Prince Bismarck and his successors.[22] None of these men, however, differed very much from Coolidge or Endicott except in having arrived at similar characteristics and values from other starting points and over distinctive routes.

More of a contrast appears if one looks instead at a very rich New York newspaper publisher—Whitelaw Reid.[23] Unlike Coolidge or Endicott, Reid came from a family of modest means and pretensions. His father, a farmer in Xenia, Ohio, had just enough capital to send Reid through nearby Miami University and afterward help him take over his home-town paper. After learning his trade in Xenia, Reid moved on to Columbus, and then, after a spell of reporting Civil War battles, to Washington.

Lean, bright-eyed, energetic, and above all ambitious,

[22] Biographical details on these men are in Burton J. Hendrick, *The Life and Letters of Andrew Carnegie*, 2 vols. (Garden City, N. Y., 1932); Chauncey M. Depew, *My Memories of Eighty Years* (New York, 1924); and Henry Villard, *Memoirs*, 2 vols. (Boston, 1904).

[23] Biographical details are in Royal Cortissoz, *The Life of Whitelaw Reid*, 2 vols. (New York, 1921). The Private Papers of Whitelaw Reid, Library of Congress, are a full and rich collection.

Reid made friends among men in positions to do him good. He had the foresight to support Lincoln over fellow Ohioan Salmon P. Chase. Once in Washington, Reid patched up relations with Chase, now Lincoln's Secretary of the Treasury, and Chase became his patron, giving him introductions to other eminent men with whom Reid also ingratiated himself.

One of Reid's conquests was Horace Greeley, the publisher of the New York *Tribune*. Though Reid represented Ohio newspapers, he wrote private letters to Greeley, offering inside information on Congressional politics. After trying unsuccessfully to make a killing as a carpetbag plantation owner in postwar Louisiana, Reid, not surprisingly, went to work for the *Tribune*, becoming within a year managing editor, and after Greeley's death, editor in chief.

Reid's abilities obviously transcended self-salesmanship. A first-class newspaperman and, even more important, a quick judge of talent in others, he kept the *Tribune* in the front rank of New York dailies. Being a good editor did not, however, account for Reid's becoming a multimillionaire. That he owed to marriage with Elisabeth Mills, only daughter of San Francisco financier Darius Ogden Mills.

Although Reid afterward owned not only the *Tribune* but also much richer properties, he continued until late in life to run the newspaper. When at his Westchester County estate, in the West, or abroad, he sent his staff explicit, detailed directives about how to allocate space, play up stories, and attune editorials. Reading them, one wonders what, if anything, he let his editors do on their own.[24]

Not having inherited or earned his fortune and retaining greater interest in his newspaper than in better-paying assets, Reid looked at the world from an angle somewhat different from that of New Yorkers who, like Coolidge in Boston, kept their minds on railroad shares or manufacturing plants. His basic values, to be sure, resembled theirs. Even before he married Elisabeth Mills he believed in the supreme importance of a sound currency and low taxes.[25] But he often held views more ambivalent than those of men primarily engaged in profit making.

Reid showed all along a sense of his country's mixed traditions. During the debate on Dominican annexation in the early 1870s he held antiexpansionist views. At the same time, remembering the Ohio of his boyhood as a frontier area and recalling how its youth had moved on to settle elsewhere, he felt that the nation might be destined still to expand and perhaps even to stretch itself into the Pacific.[26]

Similarly Reid borrowed some but not all of conventional Social Darwinism. Though certain that the American led the human species and that competitive individualism deserved the credit, he questioned whether the trend line would continue upward. Reid worried in the 1870s about corrupting effects from Irish immigration. He fretted too about the economic future, speaking in 1873 about "issues

[24] See the file of correspondence between Reid and William Seckendorff in the Reid Papers.
[25] "In an Old Ohio Town" [Feb. 16, 1881], in Reid, *American and English Studies,* 2 vols. (New York, 1913), I, 289–316.
[26] *Ibid.*

that are as grave and more complicated" than those of the Civil War era, among them "how to protect labor from capital, and how to control the corporations that absorb and dominate both." If the educated and intelligent did not exert themselves to direct affairs, he feared, the nation could easily take a turn downhill.[27] Throughout he showed something less than pure faith in the beneficial workings of natural forces.

As his words of 1873 indicate, Reid also had mixed views about the country's economic needs. His speeches and the editorial columns of the *Tribune* provide strong support for LaFeber's hypothesis. With the worsening of business conditions in 1893, the *Tribune* began to speak of the "necessity for new markets," and continued thereafter to play this theme. On the other hand, the *Tribune* and its publisher continued also to warn against big business and to protest trade expansion that would benefit only trusts. Later Reid would endorse nearly all of Theodore Roosevelt's policies and claim that the *Tribune* had been ahead of the President in advocating them. To that extent Reid might be termed a cautious pioneer progressive. In any case he did not blindly identify the good of business with the good of everyone or test public policies solely by their effects on corporate earnings.

Never having looked complacently toward the future, Reid could escape some effects of the "psychic crisis." To be sure, the Bryan campaign alarmed him. Reid's biographer says that he saw Bryan's nomination as "an impulse of

[27] *Ibid.*; Cortissoz, *Life of Whitelaw Reid*, I, 378.

the unteachable horde." [28] On the other hand, he reacted to McKinley's victory by becoming more optimistic than for two decades previously. Reid's correspondence and the editorial columns of his paper reflected continuous concern about the state of American society, but not sudden, irrational alarm.

Though sensitive to traditions, Social Darwinism, business needs, and domestic turbulence, Reid would not have adopted a view on an issue such as colonial expansion solely and simply on account of any one of these factors. All of them would have influenced him, and so too would the foreign experience that entitled him to a place in New York's foreign policy establishment.

For a long time after becoming part of his city's elite Reid had no standing as an authority on foreign affairs. Despite the *Tribune's* distinguished foreign coverage and the fact that its European correspondents sent him private reports, Reid seldom received requests, until after the mid-1880s, for his own opinion of developments abroad and how the United States should react to them. His friend and onetime employee, John Hay, who had spent several years in Europe, urged him in 1877 to seek a diplomatic appointment, writing patronizingly, "The experience of a certain world you would get, is invaluable to one whose life is sure to be passed in public such as yours is." [29]

Not following Hay's advice, Reid remained without firsthand knowledge of the foreign scene until after his

[28] *Ibid.*, II, 210.
[29] *Ibid.*, I, 364.

marriage. Then, taking a grand tour, he met Gladstone and various English leaders. In 1889, after Harrison's election, he accepted appointment as Minister to France. Remaining in Paris nearly three years, he came to know all of France's conspicuous public figures and served as host and informant on European politics to hundreds of visiting Americans. After his homecoming in 1892, his nomination as Harrison's running mate, and his return to the *Tribune* following the Republican defeat, he clearly had a new reputation. Rival papers respectfully quoted his views on foreign policy issues, and both Republican and Democratic officeholders sought his advice on such issues and his private estimates of how the public regarded them.[30]

What Reid knew and saw of Europe entered into his own opinions. Before ever crossing the Atlantic he studied developments abroad. His college work on languages had been sufficient to enable him once to consider a career as a translator of French and German works. Like others, he drew ideas about civil service and educational reform partly from observation of England. When forecasting America's future, calculating economic needs, or discussing domestic political crises, Reid referred frequently to European models. In short, one can see acting on Reid all the influences pointed out by Merk, Pratt, LaFeber, and Hofstadter—influences not only fused and intermixed but themselves colored by the additional influence that this essay seeks to

[30] The Reid Papers include an extensive clipping file and bulky folders of correspondence with Harrison, McKinley, Theodore Roosevelt, Olney, and John Hay.

64

stress: the knowledge and experience of foreign lands that formed a virtual precondition for status as a leader of opinion on foreign policy.

Somewhat the same mixture can be observed in another New Yorker whose opinions on foreign affairs the press quoted and politicians sought—Frederick William Holls.[31]

Born in 1857, the son of a Lutheran pastor recently emigrated from the Rhineland, Holls graduated from Columbia Law School to take up two careers, one as a lawyer, the other as a politician. The two sometimes intertwined, as when, in 1880, Holls asked James G. Blaine's aid in getting legal business from Depew. If free "of the drudgery of hunting up practice," Holls said, he would be able to give more time to the Republican party.[32] After marrying the daughter of a rich Rhode Islander, Holls could keep his business and his public life further apart. In the latter, though he often denied it, he aimed at supplanting the aging Carl Schurz as spokesman for German-Americans not only in New York but in the nation.

This being the case, Holls often involved himself with domestic issues. His first open contest with Schurz came in 1884. He insisted that the goals of civil service reform and honesty in government did not require German-Americans to desert the national Republican ticket. Subsequently Holls took stands in favor of international bimetallism, regulation of trusts, and federal intervention to ensure fair

[31] *In Memoriam: Frederick William Holls* (n.p., 1904); Private Papers of Frederick William Holls, Columbia University Library.
[32] Holls to Blaine, Nov. 22, 1880, Holls Papers.

65

terms of competition for small business. Even more than Reid, he could be called an anticipator of the progressive movement, and like Reid, he accepted Social Darwinism reservedly, took an ambivalent view of the nation's economic requirements, and reacted with something less than shock to domestic events of the 1890s.

In Holls's case even more than in Reid's, observation of the foreign scene formed an additional influence. With a branch law firm in Germany and German as well as American clients, he crossed the Atlantic almost every summer, and he corresponded with many German publicists and parliamentary leaders. When making political speeches to German-Americans he frequently quoted his foreign friends. Stating views on such domestic issues as civil service reform, the tariff, the currency, the need for curbing big business, and the need for conciliating labor, he drew heavily on European, particularly German, experience.[33]

Reporters and politicians asking Holls to comment on foreign policy issues probably did so in part because of his familiarity with German affairs, for international politics seemed to revolve around the Germany of Bismarck and William II. Probably Depew, Reid, and other opinion leaders asked Holls's advice for the same reasons and also because he had closer ties than they with New York's German-Americans and could give them hints as to how feeling ran within that important minority.

[33] See Holls's letter in the *Nation*, XXXI (Aug. 19, 1880), 134–135; Holls to John W. Burgess, Feb. 26, 1891, Holls Papers; Holls, "Compulsory Voting," *Annals of the American Academy of Political and Social Science*, I (1890–91), 586–614.

The examples of Reid and Holls illustrate the difficulty of generalizing about the foreign policy elite. When seeking Reid's counsel, Presidents, Secretaries of State, and senators probably wanted to take advantage of his wisdom, but they also wanted to learn what he would say, on the assumption that his views, or the *Tribune's*, would influence others. When Reid questioned Holls he probably had equally mixed motives, and Holls in turn could have sought Reid's opinions partly because he wanted his own statements to be in keeping with the eventual Republican line. Reflecting on these multiple relationships and on the fact that Reid and Holls both kept in close touch with Depew, Villard, and many others, we are reminded again of Lazarsfeld's image of "unending circuits of leadership relationships running through the community, like a nerve system through the body."

From the daily press and the correspondence of politicians and of men such as Reid and Holls one can compile a long list of New Yorkers who seemingly served as leaders of opinion. Leaving aside those who might be classified as "talkers," the list would include iron manufacturer Abram S. Hewitt, mining promoter William E. Dodge, General Horace Porter of the Pullman Company, traction magnate and Democratic party strategist William C. Whitney, Levi P. Morton, a banker who was Vice-President under Harrison and subsequently governor of New York, and Oscar S. Straus of the R. H. Macy and Abraham & Straus department stores.[34]

[34] Allan Nevins, *Abram S. Hewitt, with Some Account of Peter*

Rich and successful and, except for Dodge and Morton, college-educated, these men all had connections abroad. Hewitt claimed John Bright and Bryce as friends, and Dodge, as president of the American branch of the Evangelical Alliance, knew English churchmen and nonconformist politicians. Porter had spent many years in England representing his company. Whitney's wife, the daughter of a Standard Oil partner, had once been London correspondent for an Ohio paper, and he himself traveled often to England and bred Derby entries in association with English peers. Morton had spent four years as United States Minister in Paris, and Straus two years as Minister in Constantinople. Straus returned, as he later wrote, with the conviction that former diplomats had a duty, "by reason of their experience and standing, to inform and in a measure guide public opinion on questions concerning international affairs." [35]

Reporters and politicians consulted lawyers as well as businessmen, among them William M. Evarts, Secretary of State under Hayes and an intimate of several English law lords; Joseph H. Choate, New York's leading courtroom performer and, in England, a friend of Bright and Gladstone; and Frederick R. Coudert, a specialist in international

---

Cooper (New York, 1935); Elsie Porter Mende and Henry Greenleaf Pearson, *An American Soldier and Diplomat: Horace Porter* (New York, 1927); Mark D. Hirsch, *William C. Whitney, Modern Warwick* (New York, 1948); Private Papers of William C. Whitney, Manuscripts Division, Library of Congress; Robert McElroy, *Levi Parsons Morton* (New York, 1930); Oscar S. Straus, *Under Four Administrations* (Boston, 1922); Private Papers of Oscar S. Straus, Manuscripts Division, Library of Congress.

[35] Straus, *Under Four Administrations,* p. 105.

law, counsel in the United States for the French, Italian, and Spanish governments, and an energetic Francophile.[36]

Among editors and publishers quoted or cited in publications not their own were, besides Reid: Edwin L. Godkin of the *Evening Post* and *Nation*, an Anglo-Irishman by birth, a good friend of Bryce, James Morley, and other Gladstonian Liberals, and in the argot of the time, an Anglomane, who lauded most things English and returned to England to die; Albert Shaw of the *American Monthly Review of Reviews*, a doctor of philosophy from Johns Hopkins who had published books on municipal government in England and Europe; and Lyman Abbott of the *Outlook*, a clergyman much influenced by Darwinism, who also served as minister of Brooklyn's famous Plymouth Congregational Church, where Henry Ward Beecher had earlier preached, and who wrote and spoke on economic and social as well as religious issues and went abroad frequently to study labor conditions and welfare programs.[37]

Others playing roles as opinion leaders on foreign policy probably included Robert Stuart MacArthur of the Cal-

[36] Chester L. Barrows, *William M. Evarts, Lawyer, Diplomat, Statesman* (Chapel Hill, N. C., 1941); Edward Sanford Martin, *The Life of Joseph Hodges Choate*, 2 vols. (New York, 1920); Frederick R. Coudert, *Addresses, Historical-Political-Sociological* (New York, 1905).

[37] E. L. Godkin, *Reflection and Comments, 1865–1895* (New York, 1895); Rollo Ogden, ed., *Life and Letters of Edwin Lawrence Godkin*, 2 vols. (New York, 1907); William M. Armstrong, *E. L. Godkin and American Foreign Policy, 1865–1900* (New York, 1957); Albert Shaw, *Municipal Government in Great Britain* (New York, 1895) and *Municipal Government in Continental Europe* (New York, 1895); Lyman Abbott, *Reminiscences* (Boston, 1915); Ira V. Brown, *Lyman Abbott, Christian Evolutionist: A Study in Religious Liberalism* (Cambridge, Mass., 1953).

vary Baptist Church and R. Heber Newton of All Souls Episcopal Church; President Seth Low of Columbia University; Columbia economist Edwin R. A. Seligman; naval theorist Alfred Thayer Mahan; Irish-American lawyer and politician Bourke Cockran; and the veteran German-American leaders Schurz and General Franz Sigel.[38] Almost uniformly these men were eminent, successful, and, above all, well traveled and well connected both abroad and in Washington.

Though obviously only partial, this list suggests the diversity of New York's foreign policy elite. Nearly all, to be sure, must have known one another. Reid, for example, counted as good friends Hewitt, Morton, Whitney, Evarts, and Choate and, as we have already noted, had close political links with Depew and Holls.[39] But the group constituted no unit. It comprised strongly partisan Republicans and Democrats and also Mugwumps, such as Schurz, Godkin, and Coudert; conservatives and reformers; men who had already been prominent at the time of the Civil War and others who had come to maturity after the war; and Jews and Roman Catholics as well as Protestants. The men in it

[38] *A Service to Honor the Memory of the Rev. R. Heber Newton, D.D., and to Help Perpetuate the Ideals to Which His Life Was Dedicated* (New York, 1915); Benjamin R. C. Low, *Seth Low* (New York, 1925); José M. Pérez Cubillas, *Edwin R. A. Seligman: Estudio biográfico* (Havana, 1930); Charles Carlisle Taylor, *The Life of Admiral Mahan* (London, 1920); W. D. Puleston, *Mahan* (New Haven, 1934); James McGurrin, *Bourke Cockran, A Free Lance in American Politics* (New York, 1948); Carl Schurz, *Reminiscences,* 3 vols. (New York, 1908); Claude M. Fuess, *Carl Schurz, Reformer, 1829–1906* (New York, 1932); *DAB*, XVII, 153–154.

[39] Cortissoz, *Life of Whitelaw Reid,* I, 234–235.

did not necessarily rely on one another or enjoy equal respect in the eyes of politicians. Theodore Roosevelt regarded Depew as a "jocose beast." [40] One can imagine his feeling that if Depew said something, it must be wrong. Equally, one can imagine a partisan Republican having the same reaction to statements from prominent Mugwumps, and vice versa.

The foreign policy establishment in New York, more than that in Boston, can be visualized as a microcosm of the model of democratic behavior developed by Robert Dahl and other contemporary theorists.[41] Certain men stood out as leaders because the interested citizenry regarded them as specially well qualified. (Or at least politicians and publicists thought they were so regarded.) They had overlapping constituencies, bound to them in part by respect for their qualifications and in part by positive associations built up in the past. Thus, if Reid had a following, it probably consisted of Republicans not only conscious of his special knowledge of foreign affairs but approving, in general, of editorial lines on domestic issues taken by the *Tribune*. The stand adopted by a particular opinion leader on a particular issue took into account the stands likely to be adopted by other leaders. Any one man's stand probably reflected some conscious or unconscious judgment of what his constituency would approve. Because of idiosyncrasies or differences in background, experience, or basic belief, or differences in

[40] Elting E. Morison *et al.*, eds., *The Letters of Theodore Roosevelt*, 8 vols. (Cambridge, Mass., 1951–54), I, 582.
[41] See Robert Dahl, *A Preface to Democratic Theory* (Chicago, 1956).

the constituencies addressed, these opinion leaders might offer conflicting advice. If so, the interested public would face precisely the kind of choice that is essential to democratic process.

By focusing on leaders of opinion we do not necessarily commit ourselves to the proposition that only an elite counted. If, however, only a relatively small public concerned itself with foreign policy issues, its members would have known the special qualifications of certain individuals, and these individuals would have functioned in some sense as opinion leaders. By examining the influences working on these leaders we can perhaps come somewhat closer to understanding why opinion within the foreign policy public changed during the 1890s.

IV

THE ESTABLISHMENT: POINTS WEST AND NATIONWIDE

Iᴛ ᴡᴏᴜʟᴅ ʙᴇ unendurable to inch across the continent, compiling lists of possible opinion leaders for every urban area. Even an essay meant to be suggestive must nevertheless ask what sorts of leaders functioned in cities other than those of the East Coast and in the smaller cities more typical of urbanized America. This entails looking at two more communities—Chicago and Indianapolis.

Judged from the press and the correspondence files of public officials, Chicago's foreign policy elite appears quite similar to New York's. The city's newspapers gave no more space to the foreign policy views of local nabobs than did New York's to those of Morgan, Schiff, or Rockefeller. Not until lines on the issue were fairly clearly drawn, did they quote any multimillionaire meatpacker or industrialist as having or expressing an opinion on colonial expansion.

Early in the Philippine debate a reporter approached one merchant prince, Marshall Field. None went to Field's former partner, Levi Leiter, despite his being the father-in-law of Lord Curzon, nor to Field's other former partner, Potter Palmer, despite his having a wife who figured as a grande dame in English society. Since Field reputedly cared little about politics or public affairs or anything but business, this singling out of him could seem evidence that Chicagoans chose their opinion leaders by special criteria. But this was not necessarily so, for the occasion of Field's being questioned was his return from a long European stay.[1]

Other businessmen to whom reporters turned had credentials like those found in eastern establishments. Franklin MacVeagh, a wholesale grocer and director of the Commercial National Bank, had made many trips to Europe and considered himself an authority on European architecture. Moreover, he had a brother in Philadelphia, Wayne Mac-Veagh, who had served as United States Minister to both Turkey and Italy, had been involved in much publicized railway concession negotiations with Russia, and had belonged to the diplomatic set in Washington. Melville E. Stone, the general manager of the Associated Press, formerly publisher of the Chicago *Record*, and, with Franklin Mac-Veagh, a director of the Commercial Bank, had lived in Eu-

[1] Chicago *Tribune*, May 2, 1898; see the Earl of Ronaldshay, *The Life of Lord Curzon*, 3 vols. (London, 1928), I, 216–218; Ishbel Ross, *Silhouette in Diamonds: The Life of Mrs. Potter Palmer* (New York, 1960), pp. 39–40, 58–61; and, on Field's reputation, *DAB*, VI, 366–367.

74

rope for several years and claimed acquaintance with Gambetta, Clemenceau, and other leading foreign politicians. While Herman Henry Kohlsaat had spent abroad only the short interval between his sale of the Chicago *Inter-Ocean* and his purchase of the Chicago *Record-Herald*, he made the new paper noteworthy for its coverage of European affairs. In addition, being a close friend of McKinley's, he possessed excellent connections in Washington.[2]

Lawyers and educators treated as authorities on foreign affairs also resembled their Boston and New York counterparts. Among the lawyers were onetime State Supreme Court Justice John D. Caton, locally famed as a world traveler; Abraham Lincoln's son, Robert Todd Lincoln, counsel for the Pullman interests and, during the Harrison administration, United States Minister to Britain; Levy Mayer, who represented the Illinois Manufacturers Association and various trusts, spoke German as well as English, and lectured and wrote about international legal issues; Sigmund Zeisler, Austrian-born and educated, who led Chicago's courtroom lawyers and, in off hours, taught European law at Northwestern University; and Lambert Tree, who had been United States Minister first to Belgium and then to Russia and who at the time of his death in 1910 had crossed the Atlantic 122 times. Only one local lawyer quoted widely on foreign policy issues lacked special familiarity with Europe—federal judge Peter S. Grosscup; but

[2] For biographical details see: *DAB* (*Supplement One*), pp. 535–536 (on MacVeagh); Melville E. Stone, *Fifty Years a Journalist* (Garden City, N. Y., 1921); H. H. Kohlsaat, *From McKinley to Harding* (New York, 1923).

75

he, like Kohlsaat, could claim intimacy with McKinley.[3]

Among educators featured in the press, President William Rainey Harper of the University of Chicago had spent much time in Europe recruiting faculty; President Henry Wade Rogers of Northwestern University took an active interest in Methodist foreign missions; and historian Hermann von Holst, having left a chair at the University of Baden to join Chicago's faculty, knew Europe better than America.[4]

A profile of Chicago's foreign policy establishment—if these men were representatives of it—would differ in some respects from profiles drawn in Boston and New York. It included some men, notably Kohlsaat and Grosscup, with meager firsthand knowledge of foreign politics but with entree to the White House. More strikingly, it included no Protestant clergymen. Sermons on the colonial issue preached in Chicago churches received nothing like the feature coverage given in eastern cities to sermons by Savage, Van Ness, MacArthur, Newton, and Abbott. Even when preached by pastors of large congregations, such as Samuel Fallows and Frank W. Gunsaulus, whose words about Cuba and the crisis with Spain made front pages, they drew less attention than did sermons by Lyman Abbott of New York. One of Abbott's sermons was quoted by the *Tribune*

[3] On Caton, see *DAB*, III, 575–576; on Lincoln, *ibid.*, XI, 266–267; on Mayer, Edgar Lee Masters, *Levy Mayer and the New Industrial Era, A Biography* (New Haven, 1927); on Zeisler, *DAB*, XX, 648; on Tree, *ibid.*, XVIII, 635–636; on Grosscup, *ibid.*, VIII, 21–23.

[4] Thomas Wakefield Goodspeed, *William Rainey Harper, First President of the University of Chicago* (Chicago, 1928); on Rogers, see *DAB*, XVI, 97–98; on Von Holst, *ibid.*, IX, 177–179.

at length and used as point of departure for an editorial.[5]

Also, Chicago seemingly lacked special leaders for nationality groups. While Mayer and Von Holst had links with the German-American community, the local German-language press gave their statements on the colonial question no special play. Indeed, if one relied on a simple count of linage in the Illinois *Staatszeitung,* he would see the probable leaders of German-American opinion in Chicago as not Chicagoans at all, but Schurz, Sigel, Holls, and Representative Richard Bartholdt of St. Louis. From the *Tribune* he would infer that Chicago's large Irish community took its styles from Patrick Collins of Boston and Bourke Cockran of New York. Failing to find among themselves men whose views on foreign policy merited extraordinary respect, members of these nationality groups evidently looked for guidance to men in other cities whom they knew by reputation.

As for the smaller and more homogeneous city of Indianapolis, it too had something of a local foreign policy establishment. The Indianapolis *Journal* deferentially quoted Hugh Henry Hanna, the president of the Atlas Engine Works and also a prominent banker, who had studied in Germany and subsequently won a national reputation as an authority on international monetary affairs.[6] Both the *Journal* and the Indianapolis *News* gave play to statements by two lawyers, Albert J. Beveridge and John Lewis

[5] Chicago *Tribune,* May 5, 1898.
[6] *Who's Who in America, 1914–1915,* p. 1023; New York *Journal of Commerce,* Feb. 1, 1898.

Griffiths. The former, though only in his mid-thirties in 1898, already had nationwide fame as an orator. Having toured Europe in 1894 and sent back to the *News* reports of interviews with famous generals, he seemingly possessed special knowledge of foreign military affairs. In addition, though it may not have been public knowledge, he exchanged letters on foreign policy issues with, among others, Chicago's Representative Robert R. Hitt, Chairman of the House Foreign Affairs Committee, Theodore Roosevelt, Lodge, Depew, and Albert Shaw.[7] Griffiths, Beveridge's chief local competitor in oratory, had never been outside the United States but had made a hobby of studying English literature and history and following English politics. He could cite chapter and verse of Joseph Chamberlain's accomplishments as mayor of Birmingham.[8]

Though former President Benjamin Harrison lived in Indianapolis, the local press did not treat him as a leader of opinion. Statements by him that made news nationally attracted no more notice in Indianapolis than elsewhere. Indeed, when Harrison was visited in May 1898 by his former Secretary of State, international lawyer John W. Foster, Indianapolis reporters talked with both and then featured

[7] Claude G. Bowers, *Beveridge and the Progressive Era* (Boston, 1932); Indianapolis *News*, April 17, May 8, 1898; Indianapolis *Journal*, April 17, Sept. 17, 1898; Private Papers of Albert J. Beveridge, Library of Congress.

[8] *The Greater Patriotism: Public Addresses by John Lewis Griffiths, American Consul General at London, Delivered in England and America, with a Memoir by Caroline Henderson Griffiths and an Introduction by Hilaire Belloc* (London, 1918); Indianapolis *Journal*, May 8, July 5, 1898.

Foster's statements rather than Harrison's, even though both men spoke noncommittally.[9]

More than to Harrison, or for that matter, Hanna, Beveridge, or Griffiths, Indianapolis newspapers looked to General Lew Wallace for newsworthy statements on foreign policy issues. A Civil War hero and author of *Ben-Hur*, Wallace had served as Minister to Turkey in the early 1880s. Having observed and reported the British seizure of Egypt, he retained thereafter a strong interest in British colonial policy. Knowing that fact and knowing also that Presidents, Secretaries of State, and senators from Indiana and other states sought Wallace's counsel, reporters hunted for him when Hawaii and the Philippines were on the front pages. He could not appear in a railroad station or hotel in Indianapolis without becoming copy, even when he declined to comment.[10]

Compared with Boston, New York, or Chicago, Indianapolis had only a handful of potential opinion leaders. But it did have that handful. As a state capital and major railroad junction, it was not, of course, typical of cities with a population under 250,000. One cannot reason that every other such city had its Hanna, Beveridge, Griffiths, and Wallace. One can, however, reason that at least a few must have had counterparts.

Also, we probably have to assume that our quick survey

[9] Indianapolis *Journal*, May 4 and 8, 1898; Indianapolis *News*, May 8, 1898.

[10] Indianapolis *Journal*, Jan. 30, 1893, May 7 and 21, June 5, 1898; see Irving McKee, *"Ben-Hur" Wallace, The Life of General Lew Wallace* (Berkeley, Calif., 1947), esp. pp. 200–217, 233–234, 250–258.

79

has missed many influential figures. Of some we find traces and nothing more—the Reverend Thomas Craven, whom the Chicago *Inter-Ocean* mentioned casually as "one of the best informed men in the country about Eastern affairs," and Smiley N. Chambers of Indianapolis, whom the *Journal* characterized as "a citizen eminently qualified" to discuss the colonial issue.[11] Many others must have failed to catch the notice of reporters and must have communicated with politicians by word of mouth or in letters that have not survived.

Of one such man we have more than a trace. For over twenty years Ellis Yarnall, a Philadelphia manufacturer, carried on a regular correspondence with Sir John Coleridge (eventually Lord Coleridge), the son of the poet and at one time England's Lord Chief Justice.[12] These letters show Yarnall acting as an opinion guide for Philadelphians a good deal more prominent than he: his "warm friend," Wayne MacVeagh; William H. Rawle, the city's foremost lawyer; Franklin Gowen, president of the Reading Railroad; Alexander J. Cassatt, president of the Pennsylvania; and historian and real estate developer Henry C. Lea. Not only corresponding with Coleridge but also subscribing to the London *Times*, visiting England regularly, and being introduced by Coleridge to English political leaders, Yarnall remained better informed than his friends about events

11 Chicago *Inter-Ocean*, Aug. 10, 1898; Indianapolis *Journal*, July 5, 1898.

12 Charlton Yarnall, ed., *Forty Years of Friendship, as Recorded in the Correspondence of John Duke, Lord Coleridge and Ellis Yarnall During the Years 1856 to 1895* (London, 1911), *passim*.

abroad. Yet it was to MacVeagh, Rawle, Gowen, Cassatt, and Lea that reporters went for comment on foreign affairs. Probably Yarnall had counterparts in other big cities and perhaps also in smaller communities such as Indianapolis.

Labeling these men and more visible figures, such as Coolidge and Reid, as "opinion leaders" involves at least as much ambiguity as labeling Cleveland, McKinley, or Theodore Roosevelt "political leaders." No man among them could stride forward on his own, confident that large numbers would blindly follow. Such correspondence files as we possess indicate that they constantly consulted one another not just to ascertain the views of others but also to learn the mood of the interested citizenry. And, of course, politicians sought the same of them—not just wisdom but also indications of what portion of the public might become concerned, how intensely, and with what leanings. Opinion leaders might offer guidance to the public, but seldom without making sure that other leaders would point similar courses and that the headings would appeal to at least some interested citizens.

Even in a restricted sense, however, we have to speak of some men as national opinion leaders. Newspapers throughout the country gave publicity to statements by Olney, Carnegie, Depew, Reid, Straus, Choate, Coudert, Abbott, Godkin, Shaw, Mahan, Lincoln, and Von Holst. Irish-American and German-American periodicals all over the nation treated Collins, Cockran, Schurz, Sigel, and Holls as their own. Dailies in Boston, New York, and Chicago quoted not only members of each other's establishments but also men from other localities, such as former Secretary of State Thomas F. Bayard of Delaware, Wayne MacVeagh, Don Dickinson of Michigan, Clark Howell of the Atlanta *Constitution*, and railroad magnate Leland Stanford of California. Senators such as Lodge, William E. Chandler of New Hampshire, Orville Platt of Connecticut, Johnson N. Camden of New Jersey, Shelby M. Cullom of Illinois, Cushman K. Davis of Minnesota, and William B. Allison of Iowa wrote to men of this stripe for advice. An intricate national network linked local circuits of opinion leadership, and the existence of this network multiplied the varieties of opinion in circulation and hence the opportunities for choice on the part of attentive citizens.

The extent of choice depended to some extent on disagreement within the establishment. While personal and partisan differences ensured a certain amount of discord, the fact that members of the establishment so much resembled one another made a certain amount of consensus equally inevitable. To be sure, nothing could prevent men of any condition or persuasion from putting opinions into the market. Semiliterate farmers or workers could publish letters in agricultural or labor weeklies, if nowhere else, and radicals could seize space in dailies by delivering speeches in public parks. The potential following for such would-be leaders within the foreign policy public could only be small, however, so long as they had no backers with the cachet of success and social status, reputation for good judgment, special knowledge, foreign experience, and connections in Washington. While no individual member of the establishment could really lead, in the sense of dictating opinion to a segment of the public, the establishment could determine collectively the terms on which any foreign policy debate would be conducted.

While members of the establishment might take careful account of their potential constituents, they could not, any more than politicians, choose their stands solely to win popularity, for they could know in advance only the extreme limits of what their constituency might approve or disapprove. Faced with a situation calling for comment, members of the establishment had to act as leaders. In doing so they had to legitimize their positions by reference to some standard other than the public will.

Convention, tradition, or precedent formed the most convenient such standard. Whether conservatives or reformers, the men of the establishment believed to the depths of their being that past generations of Americans had built well and beautifully. Even those who thought improvements in order were in some sense conservatives, and almost without exception, they knew a good deal about America's political heritage. The speeches of Olney, Depew, Reid, Holls, Von Holst, Beveridge, and others display astonishingly detailed knowledge of the words and acts of the founding fathers and statesmen of the Webster-Clay-Calhoun epoch. Confronted with a question about what the country ought to do in a given situation, the typical member of the establishment would probably have thought immediately of what had transpired on some past occasion.

Possible precedents coming to mind might include many

83

besides those which would occur to less learned men. Facing a question to do with colonies, a member of the establishment would almost certainly think of Manifest Destiny as well as the anticolonial tradition. Depending on which side of the issue he supported, he might defend his choice by reference either to the precedents of Florida, Louisiana, and California or to the decision not to annex all of Mexico, the protest against extension of slavery, and the rejection of Grant's proposal for annexation of the Dominican Republic. For some, of course, the precedents that seemed relevant would be, at least in part, determinative. For others the significant fact would be only that the precedents permitted a choice and provided a defense for an opinion arrived at by other means. Nevertheless, looking at the establishment, one sees more clearly how the influence emphasized by Merk may have come into play.

Another "objective" standard for members of the establishment might have been the scientific wisdom of the time. Certainly John Fiske and Andrew Carnegie respected Social Darwinism. So did reformist clergymen, such as Minot Savage and Lyman Abbott. For most, however, Social Darwinist teachings added up to little more than affirmation of Longfellow's warning that life was real and earnest. Men like Coolidge, Olney, Depew, Reid, Holls, Choate, Kohlsaat, and Robert Todd Lincoln could hardly have felt confident about an opinion solely because it found sanction in Herbert Spencer. For most members of the establishment, and hence for most of the foreign policy public, the sense of America's mixed historical tradition probably

84

played a more important role than Social Darwinism in determining and legitimizing opinions.

The same cannot be said of economic considerations. Business conditions interested nearly all the men we have discussed. Even for those with little directly at stake, such as Fiske, Mahan, and Von Holst, economic indices measured the nation's health. Conviction that a given policy would benefit or harm the economy could control their views. In any case, given the general acceptance, by farmers and workers no less than businessmen, of the need for expanded exports, an argument from that need provided obvious packaging for any opinion ventured into the market place.

Economic reasoning could, of course, lead to more than one conclusion about colonies. Cotton, wheat, beef, pork, minerals, and manufactures such as woven textiles and steel rails seemed in greatest oversupply, and the likeliest buyers for these products were in Europe, Latin America, and China rather than in places where America might acquire colonies. Many people felt that by taking tropical colonies the United States would antagonize Europeans and alarm Latin Americans and Chinese and thus lose rather than gain the markets it needed. Economic considerations provided a standard for members of the establishment, but, like historical tradition, a standard that was flexible rather than fixed.

As for the "psychic crisis," it would have influenced members of the establishment much as did Social Darwinism. Kohlsaat could come out for war with Spain in 1898, saying "Our own internal political conditions will not permit its

85

postponement. . . . 'war for Cuban liberty' looms before us as the only rallying standard for the legions of our national discontent." [13] Meditating the colonial issue, he and others may well have had similar thoughts. Such fears could seldom be brought forward, however, as the legitimizing basis for a policy recommendation.

Tradition and economic considerations thus held first place among the sources of authority on which members of the establishment could base their stands. Social Darwinist concepts held an equal place only for a few. While a "psychic crisis" may have been a private influence, it did not serve the same purposes as tradition and economic reasoning.

Ranking with these latter, however, was the observed experience of other nations. In explaining why he came to a particular policy stand, a member of the establishment might be chary of citing alleged scientific rules and charier still of adducing the disturbed state of the public mind, but he could readily refer to history, to the needs of American business, *and* to what had happened or was said to have happened abroad.

As we have already observed repeatedly, the men who seemed to function as opinion leaders nearly all had close firsthand knowledge of Europe. The few who knew other parts of the globe formed a minority, and almost no one otherwise equipped to be a community leader knew the Far East, Africa, or even Latin America without having at least

[13] Ernest R. May, *Imperial Democracy: The Emergence of America as a Great Power* (New York, 1961), p. 146.

comparable knowledge of Europe.[14] The men asked by the press and politicians for guidance on colonial expansion were, *faute de mieux*, men who knew most about colonies as topics of debate in European capitals.

Looking at the American press throughout the decade, one can infer that something more than lack of choice was involved—that the foreign policy public regarded European experience as a no less valid guide for the United States than, for example, the country's own historic traditions. On the question of whether the United States should acquire colonies, newspapers gave extraordinary coverage to statements by Englishmen. When Henry Norman, the editor of the London *Daily Chronicle*, published an article on the subject, its text was cabled to the United States and

---

[14] The Boston *Globe*, Jan. 29, 1893, printed interviews with thirteen men who had lived in Hawaii. In the special circumstances, some of these thirteen may have been looked to for opinion guidance. The fact that all favored annexation conceivably had some influence. But none had markedly high standing in the community. Through the Harvard College Library index to Boston *Evening Transcript* obituaries, it was possible to find notices of James F. Hunnewell, a writer of travel books (Nov. 12, 1910), E. P. Bond, a missionary (Feb. 11, 1893), and three businessmen, S. C. Armstrong (May 12, 1893), Charles Brewer (Oct. 24, 1904), and Gorham D. Gilman (Oct. 4, 1909). If the others—E. P. Adams, James W. Austin, H. A. P. Carter, J. N. Lindsey, C. N. Lunt, J. F. B. Marshall, D. M. Weston, and R. W. Wood—died in or near Boston, the *Transcript* took no note. Most cities had no comparable local group. New York, Philadelphia, and Chicago papers could find no more than one or two local residents who knew Hawaii at first hand. Along with reports of their views, these papers printed stories from Boston, repeating copy from the *Globe*. While one need not assume that words from these various old Hawaii hands were totally without weight, still it is evident that no community, except possibly San Francisco, had even a local group qualified to guide opinion on foreign policy and specially acquainted with the Pacific area.

87

printed, as a full column or more, in the Philadelphia *North American*, the Chicago *Inter-Ocean*, and the Indianapolis *Journal*.[15] Both the New York *World* and the Chicago *Inter-Ocean* gave first-page coverage to statements by Sir Charles Dilke and another M.P., Henry Howarth. The *World* justified this placement of the story by describing Howarth as "a leading authority on foreign politics." [16] The New Orleans *Times-Picayune*, which in May 1898 reported comment on the Philippine question by no local citizen, gave a full column to an interview with Edward Potter, an obscure English businessman who happened to be passing through the city. The Chicago *Tribune* devoted comparable space to an interview with Amyas Northcote, the young son of a Conservative peer.[17]

All this suggests that American editors—and, by implication, the interested American public—viewed the issues confronting the United States as comparable to issues that Europeans had faced. In an editorial printed alongside the interview with Northcote the Chicago *Tribune* said as much. Knowing a great deal about European politics, the *Tribune* observed, Northcote was "peculiarly qualified to advise us on the new questions which have been raised by the war."

To explain why the interested public as well as the establishment should have attached so much importance to Eu-

[15] Philadelphia *North American*, May 30, 1898; Chicago *Inter-Ocean*, June 1, July 1, 1898; Indianapolis *Journal*, May 30, 1898.

[16] New York *World*, May 9, 1898; Chicago *Inter-Ocean*, May 10, 1898.

[17] New Orleans *Times-Picayune*, May 2, 1898; Chicago *Tribune*, May 11, 1898.

ropean experience and to the views of Englishmen and Europeans, one must bear in mind not only America's cultural dependence but also the fact that a relatively large public knew something of Europe. E. L. Godkin wrote:

> There is probably no American who has risen above very narrow circumstances who does not go to Europe at least once in his life. There is hardly a village in the country in which the man who has succeeded in trade or commerce does not announce his success to his neighbors by a trip to Europe for himself and his family. There is hardly a professor, or teacher, or clergyman, or artist, or author who does not save out of a salary, however small, in order to make the voyage.[18]

Though Godkin overstated the truth, he did not misstate it. One can hardly find a biography or autobiography of a late-nineteenth-century American that does not mention at least one trip abroad. The more affluent a man, the more often he went. John Wanamaker, the Philadelphia department store owner, writes of having contracted "the habit of Europe." The far western railroad and mining kings made the journey as often as eastern millionaires. And, as Godkin commented, many others traveled on the same steamships. In 1897, 2,000 Americans attended the annual Fourth of July party at the United States embassy in Paris.[19]

[18] E. L. Godkin, *Reflections and Comments, 1865–1895* (New York, 1895), pp. 281–282.

[19] Herbert Adams Gibbon, *John Wanamaker,* 2 vols. (New York, 1926), II, 49; Joseph Gilpin Pyle, *The Life of James J. Hill,* 2 vols. (Gar-

Visits of foreigners to America furthered acquaintance with England and Europe. Though they came from all parts, including Russia, Germans and Englishmen predominated. The German utilities magnate Georg von Siemens and the National Liberal party leaders Johannes Miquel and Eduard Lasker made highly publicized tours.[20] From England came both titled aristocrats and members of governments. Rosebery built up his circle of American friends during several long stays in New York and shorter stays in Pennsylvania and Illinois.[21] Joseph Chamberlain came to the United States while a cabinet minister. Courting Mary Endicott, he met many members of Boston and Washington society, and Chauncey Depew introduced him to New York's business leaders.[22] The intensity of interest in these visitors is suggested by Lady Randolph Churchill's recollection of being mobbed when she and her husband descended from a train in San Francisco in 1894.[23]

---

den City, 1917), II, 407, 480; Oscar Lewis, *The Big Four: The Story of Huntington, Stanford, Hopkins, and Crocker, and of the Building of the Central Pacific* (New York, 1938), pp. 271–272, and *Silver Kings* (New York, 1947), pp. 77–111; Esie Porter Mende and Henry Greenleaf Pearson, *An American Soldier and Diplomat, Horace Porter* (New York, 1927), p. 187.

[20] Alfred Vagts, *Deutschland und die Vereinigten Staaten in der Weltpolitik*, 2 vols. (New York, 1935), I, 430–442.

[21] The Marquess of Crewe, *Lord Rosebery*, 2 vols. (London, 1931), I, 66–76, 79–82, 88–90, 95–96, 175–176; Robert Rhodes James, *Rosebery* (London, 1963), p. 69.

[22] J. L. Garvin, *The Life of Joseph Chamberlain*, 3 vols. (London, 1932–34), II, 327–334, 402; Sir Willoughby Maycock, *With Mr. Chamberlain in the United States and Canada, 1887–88* (Toronto, n.d.).

[23] Mrs. George Cornwallis-West, *The Reminiscences of Lady Randolph Churchill* (New York, 1908), pp. 314–315.

Mention of Chamberlain and Randolph Churchill calls attention to the role of American women in stimulating interest in the world beyond the continental limits. When, as in these two instances, eminent foreigners married American women, American newspapers not only devoted extensive space to the wedding ceremonies but also paid special attention to the careers of the husbands. Among these husbands, in addition to Chamberlain, Churchill, and Lord Curzon, were: in England, William Vernon Harcourt and his son, Lewis (Loulou), Sir Arthur Paget, Michael Herbert, Moreton Frewen, Lyon Playfair, Benjamin Conn Costelloe, and aristocrats such as the Dukes of Manchester and Marlborough and the Earl of Essex; in France, onetime Foreign Minister William Henry Waddington, Alexandre Ribot, and from the worlds of high finance and high society, Baron Hottinguer, the Duc de Praslin, the Marquis de Talleyrand, and Comte Sartiges.[24]

Some of these American wives did more than simply call attention to their husbands. Mrs. Chamberlain assisted her husband's campaigns, and Lady Randolph Churchill helped organize the Primrose League. A number who simply took an active interest in their husbands' affairs talked with American friends or wrote home about the politics of their adopted countries. Lady Curzon and Mary King Wadding-

[24] Ignota, "Charming Links in the Anglo American Alliance," *Harmsworth's* (London, Sept. 1898), as summarized in *Review of Reviews*, XVIII (Oct. 1898), 523. Mary King Waddington, *My First Years as a Frenchwoman, 1876–1879* (New York, 1914), p. 192; Cornwallis-West, *Reminiscences of Lady Randolph Churchill*, pp. 39, 60, 399; Chicago *Tribune*, June 20, 1898.

ton, for example, appear to have carried on a large corre-spondence with Americans.[25] One suspects that some of these women may have married as they did in part because opportunities to take part in high politics seemed surer in England or France than in the United States. In any case their service as connecting links between the continents ought not to be overlooked.

Acquaintance with Europe was most common, of course, in those circles that could be described as "high society." In *The Bread-Winners*, his novel of Cleveland, John Hay says of "the brightest and gayest young girls" that "they had all had their seasons in Paris and in Washington. . . . They nearly all spoke French and German better than they did English." [26] While the attention of such girls and their fami-lies may have centered chiefly on who wore what, went where, and married whom, interest nevertheless extended well beyond these circles and these subjects.

Newspaper publishers and editors judged all along that their readers wanted a great deal of information about Eu-rope. The New York *Herald* sent twenty-four correspond-ents to cover the Franco-Prussian war. In subsequent years competition between the *Herald* and the New York *Trib-une* focused mainly on the quality of reportage from Lon-don and Paris. The same held true in Chicago. The Chicago *Tribune*, having established a London bureau in 1877,

25 Ronaldshay, *Life of Lord Curzon*, I, 216–218, 220–221; Waddington, *My First Years as a Frenchwoman*, p. 77, and *Letters of a Diplomat's Wife* (New York, 1903), *passim*.
26 Anon. [John Hay], *The Bread-Winners: A Social Study* (New York, 1884), p. 174.

trumpeted its claim to the best foreign coverage in the West. When Melville Stone founded the competing *Morning News* in the 1890s, he gave primary attention to building up a corps of foreign correspondents better than the *Tribune's*, and Kohlsaat, after taking over the *Record-Herald*, set his eyes on the same goal.[27] From an analysis of the New York *Tribune*, the Chicago *Tribune*, and the Boston *Evening Transcript*, Arthur M. Schlesinger calculates that of space devoted to political news, the proportion going to foreign politics was 40.3 per cent in 1878, 15.4 per cent in 1888, and 26.0 per cent in 1898.[28]

Until Pulitzer and Hearst showed how to build circulation by sensationalism, metropolitan dailies reached relatively select audiences. Pulitzer's *World*, in 1888, became the first to sell as many as 250,000 copies.[29] Most dailies thus addressed the comparatively prosperous and educated, and editors obviously judged readers to be interested in people and events abroad.

Many signs of this interest existed. Josiah Benton, a former Vermont farm boy practicing law in Boston, had three pictures on the wall behind his desk. On one side appeared the president of the Old Colony railroad, on the other a leader of the Boston bar, and in the center Prince Bismarck. After visiting New York, Cecil Spring Rice

[27] Stone, *Fifty Years a Journalist*, pp. 108–109; John Hohenberg, *Foreign Correspondence: The Great Reporters and Their Times* (New York, 1964), pp. 77, 86–92.

[28] Arthur M. Schlesinger, *The Rise of the City, 1878–1898* (New York, 1933), p. 199. The author cites an unpublished study by B. B. Bouton.

[29] *Ibid.*, p. 189, n. 2.

wrote, "It is absurd how well everyone here seems to know everything that goes on in London. Lord Rosebery seems as well known here as in England." Lord Russell of Killowen recorded of Mike McDonald, a Chicago gambler and ward boss, "He shows great knowledge of European politics, or at least those of France and Great Britain." [30] Familiarity with political currents in the Old World was not confined to high society.

In tracing the development of American attitudes toward imperialism this fact must be taken into account. It explains in part why the foreign policy public would have looked for guidance to Coolidge, Reid, Holls, and their like. Knowing that Englishmen, Frenchmen, and Germans had debated issues very like those facing Americans in Hawaii and the Philippines, members of this public would have turned to men well informed about what had been said and done abroad. In addition, having followed foreign politics in the press and perhaps seen Europe at first hand, many of these Americans could have been themselves influenced by European experience. It thus joins tradition, economic interest, scientific dogma, and psychological distress as a factor that may have shaped views within the interested public.

[30] Samuel Leland Powers, *Portraits of a Half Century* (Boston, 1925), p. 72; Stephen Gwynn, ed., *The Letters and Friendships of Sir Cecil Spring Rice: A Record*, 2 vols. (London, 1929), I, 58; R. Barry O'Brien, *The Life of Lord Russell of Killowen* (London, 1901), pp. 162–163.

V

THE ANTI-IMPERIALIST
TRADITION

EVEN A SKETCH of English and European influence on
American thought about colonies has to go back to the
1860s. As Richard Koebner has shown, the word "imperialism" came into the English language in that era. Con-
cocted to describe the Second Empire of Napoleon III, it
meant rule by a despot who drew his power from popularity with the masses. Because of policies associated with both
Napoleons the word also connoted expansionism, and increasingly, after Napoleon III's expedition to Indochina and
support of Maximilian in Mexico, conquests giving the
home country control over less developed lands and races.[1]

[1] Richard Koebner and Helmut Dan Schmitt, *Imperialism: The Story
and Significance of a Political Word, 1840–1960* (Cambridge, Eng., 1964),
pp. 1–26.

Liberals everywhere censured imperialism in each of its successive meanings. With local variations, liberals of this era attributed progress to free competition, unhindered by state interference. Partly because they believed in political equality, but doubted that mass electorates would conserve and expand individual liberties, they insisted on weak governments, subject to constitutions stipulating a division of powers. In liberal eyes the Second Empire compounded its wrongs by attempting to expand. Liberals believed acquisition of new possessions and zones of influence interfered with natural economic processes and, by creating new revenues and patronage and new needs for soldiers and warships, increased the power of the state, added to the popularity of the dictator, and delayed progress toward proper constitutionalism. The example of Napoleon III thus made colonial expansion anathema to liberals.

This new point of liberal dogma drew further support from the view then current of relations between Great Britain and the United States. Not only did the United States seem much more vigorous than the portion of North America that had remained British but it purchased more British products and borrowed more capital. The inference followed that even such light rule as England exercised in Canada impeded progress.

Some English liberals concluded that their country ought to get rid of its empire. As C. A. Bodelson has shown, even Tories believed Canada should become independent.[2] And

[2] C. A. Bodelson, *Studies in Mid-Victorian Imperialism* (Copenhagen, 1924), pp. 42–52.

the speakers and writers most loudly voicing liberal anti-colonialism happened to be also the Englishmen most attractive to Americans, or at least to Americans in northern cities.

One such was Goldwin Smith. Regius Professor of Modern History at Oxford, Smith became emotionally involved in the American Civil War, championing the North. In 1863, with the war at its height, he published a book of essays, *The Empire*, depicting England's greatest future interest as friendship and trade with the United States.[3] The British government would best serve this interest, Smith argued, by transferring Canada to the American republic, thus at once acknowledging the geographical and cultural unity between the Canadian provinces and the Union and removing a potential source of Anglo-American friction. Reaching Americans when their nation's very survival stood in doubt, Smith's essays had greater impact and appeal than they might have had at a cooler time. Though their message could be received with pleasure by a believer in Manifest Destiny, they helped to establish a further association between pride in America on the one hand and a low appreciation of colonies on the other.

The example and teaching of John Bright reinforced this association. One of the great orators of the House of Commons, Bright had long lent support to American abolitionists, and during the Civil War, he had been a conspicuous

[3] Goldwin Smith, *The Empire, A Series of Letters Published in "The Daily News"* (Oxford, 1863); see Bodelson, *Mid-Victorian Imperialism*, pp. 52–57, and Elisabeth Wallace, *Goldwin Smith: Victorian Liberal* (Toronto, 1957).

friend of the Union. Though Bright espoused other causes, not all of which enraptured all Americans (free trade being the outstanding example), he was said to be "the most popular man in America" and told that if he crossed the Atlantic, Americans "would scatter flowers before him all the way from Chicago to the sea." [4] The fact that he, like Smith, argued in principle against colonies and described Canada's destiny as union with the United States must have carried weight with his American admirers.

Scarcely five years after Appomattox, with liberal anticolonialism at its apogee in England and Louis Napoleon's failure in Mexico a fresh memory, President Grant put before the American public the issue of whether or not to acquire a colonial empire. He proposed annexing the Dominican Republic.

Prior to the war the free state-slave state division had prevented Americans from discussing territorial expansion on its own merits.[5] Immediately afterward a treaty for the purchase of Alaska from Russia caused such discussion to commence. Though the Senate ratified the treaty almost instantly, the House of Representatives provided opportunity for public debate by waiting a year to appropriate the necessary money. In the meantime Secretary of State William

[4] R. A. J. Walling, ed., *The Diaries of John Bright* (New York, 1931), p. 297; George Macaulay Trevelyan, *The Life of John Bright* (Boston, 1913), p. 327; J. Travis Mills, *John Bright and the Quakers*, 2 vols. (London, 1935), II, 217–223.

[5] See Basil Rauch, *American Interest in Cuba, 1848–1855* (New York, 1948). In Albert K. Weinberg, *Manifest Destiny* (Baltimore, 1935), pp. 65–67, 153–154, 196–202, 205–210, 230–235, this point is evident but not treated explicitly.

H. Seward negotiated another treaty, this one with Denmark, providing for purchase of St. Thomas and St. John in the Danish West Indies (now the Virgin Islands).

The Alaskan bargain aroused both opposition and support. Picturing the territory as a frozen waste, critics spoke of "Seward's folly" and "Seward's ice box" and the extravagance of spending $7,500,000 on it when costs of war and reconstruction remained unpaid. In the end, backers of the purchase won, but only by arguing that Russia had been friendly to the Union and would be offended if America reneged and by paying cash bribes to key legislators. But no opponent said the United States ought not to expand. On the contrary, everyone accepted the rightness and inevitability of America's engrossing the northern part of the continent, including Canada. Dispute concerned solely the price of the particular tract.[6]

Only when Congress and the interested public turned to the Danish islands and the Dominican Republic, did a matter of principle arise. Possessing a small, mostly North European population, St. Thomas and St. John presented a new issue only because they lay a thousand miles away from the continent. In addition to being distant and bounded by water, the Dominican Republic was a tropical land with little space left for settlement and already peopled by 100,000 to 200,000 Spaniards, mulattoes, and Negroes different in cultural background from the majority of

---

[6] The most convenient summary is that of Joe Patterson Smith, *The Republican Expansionists of the Early Reconstruction Era* (Chicago, 1933).

99

Americans. With a Cuban war for independence in progress and some Americans agitating for intervention, it seemed conceivable that a decision to take the Dominican Republic might lead to other steps, making much of the Caribbean the property of the United States. Some Americans felt that the nation faced a fundamental choice between, on the one hand, organic growth such as had been the pattern in the past and, on the other, expansion by incorporation of alien tribes, after the fashion of the Romans.

Others saw annexation of the Dominican Republic as no departure from precedent. Leading the fight in the Senate for ratification of President Grant's treaty, Republicans Roscoe Conkling of New York, Oliver P. Morton of Indiana, and James W. Nye of Nevada laid heavy stress on the tradition of Manifest Destiny. Nathaniel P. Banks of Massachusetts and Godlove Orth of Indiana, making proannexation speeches in the House, asked Democratic members how they could oppose a measure which, though sponsored by a Republican administration, had a heritage reaching back to Jefferson, Madison, Jackson, and Polk. Fernando Wood of New York, speaking for House Democrats, confessed that it caused him pain to oppose and that he did so only because annexation would add to the country's Negro population.[7]

Other foes of the treaty, however, alleged that past expansion had involved natural growth as a free, Protestant, and Nordic nation. Representative John F. Farnsworth of

[7] 41 Cong., 3 sess., *Congressional Globe*, pp. 237-239, 244-245, 385-388, 406-416.

Illinois denounced his colleagues for even thinking of invit-
ing "semi-civilized, semi-barbarous men who cannot speak
our language, who are unused to our laws and institutions,
to vote with us, to help legislate for us." According to
newspaper accounts, Senator Charles Sumner of Massachusetts opposed the treaty in executive session on the
ground that the nation's great heritage would be menaced
by "taking into this country any of the Latin race, with its
treacherous blood and its notions of superstition and big-
otry." Both Sumner and Carl Schurz, then a senator from
Missouri, argued that Manifest Destiny ran only on the
continent and that expansion beyond the water's edge
would involve dangers such as the republic had never faced
before.[8]

Both sides invoked economic considerations. In recom-
mending the treaty, Grant had described the Dominican
Republic as "one of the richest territories under the sun,"
possessing "the richest soil, best and most capacious har-
bors, most salubrious climate, and the most valuable products of the forests, mines, and soil of any of the West
India Islands." To acquire it, he said, "is to furnish new
markets for the products of our farms, shops, and manufac-
tories." [9] All champions of the treaty echoed his words, emphasizing almost invariably the potential richness of the

[8] 41 Cong., 2 sess., *Congressional Globe*, p. 4437; *New York Times*,
March 14, 1870; 41 Cong., 3 sess., *Congressional Globe*, pp. 226–231;
Frederic Bancroft, ed., *Speeches, Correspondence and Political Papers of
Carl Schurz*, 6 vols. (New York, 1913), II, 109–111.

[9] James D. Richardson, ed., *A Compilation of the Messages and Papers
of the Presidents*, 12 vols. (n.p., 1908), VII, 61–63.

Dominican Republic as a place for settlement and for farming and mining and arguing vigorously that it would provide an outlet for agricultural exports. Representative Morton S. Wilkinson of Minnesota said, "We western men are entitled to the market of Cuba and of the Gulf of Mexico. That market belongs to us, and whenever we can get it legitimately and properly . . . we ought to lay our hands upon it and take it." [10] Not surprisingly, much less was said of Dominicans as potential customers for American factory products. As LaFeber would point out, American industrialists did not yet fear producing more than the domestic population could consume.

On the antiannexation side, the economic argument started with a denial of Grant's proposition. The Dominican Republic, said Sumner and Schurz, had no room for American farmers and would offer them a cold welcome if they came; its mineral riches already belonged to speculators with early inside knowledge of the annexation negotiations. To Americans at large, the senators asserted, annexation would simply mean more expense—for a navy to defend the new territory, for spoilsmen to administer it, and for troops to provide order.

In Congress, supporters and opponents of the President's project did not divide along sectional lines. Regardless of where they came from, most Democrats opposed the policy of the Republican administration. While a number of pro-annexation Republicans represented the Midwest or Far West, Banks and Benjamin Butler both came from Massa-

[10] 41 Cong., 2 sess., *Congressional Globe*, p. 492.

chusetts. The clearest division among Republicans lay between men identified and not identified with Grant. Roll calls on the relevant Senate and House votes showed lines running between parties and intraparty factions.

The nature of the debaters' points scored by the two sides nevertheless differed. Proponents of annexation couched their case to appeal to men with only a crude sense of the nation's history. They relied on evoking emotions associated with catchwords and with such names as Jefferson and Jackson. They addressed their economic arguments to restless and conceivably land-hungry farmers and workingmen.

Opponents of annexation addressed a somewhat different public. In speaking of tradition, Farnsworth, Sumner, and Schurz invoked abstractions rather than concrete symbols. They appealed to fear of change and to the economic interests of the relatively small group conscious of paying taxes.

From the Congressional debates one could draw the conclusion that members of the two houses expected proannexation and antiannexation opinion to divide along economic or social lines. It may have been, of course, that support for Grant ran strongest among workingmen, poor farmers, and unsettled young war veterans, or that politicians with such constituencies most needed Grant's coattails. Even so, however, supporters of annexation need not have spoken as they did solely because the project was the President's.

At least one proannexationist expected expansion in and of itself to be popular with the relatively disadvantaged.

Banks, known as "the bobbin boy" because of beginning as a child laborer in a cotton mill, owed his power in Massachusetts to a following among mill-town workers and, despite once being a Know-Nothing, among Boston's Irish immigrants. Service as a general during the war had taken him away from the state, and he returned to find his political base shaky. According to his biographer, Fred Harvey Harrington, he seized upon expansionism in the belief that it would restore his prospects of becoming governor or senator. "I want to identify my name . . . ," Banks wrote to his wife, "with the acquisition of the Gulf of *Mexico* as a Sea of the United States." [11]

If Banks and others expected workers and immigrants to rally to such a standard, opponents of annexation must have expected some other groups to respond differently. No fewer than twenty-one Republican senators voted against Grant's treaty. Most advertised the fact by speaking against annexation in open sessions, and some sought unsuccessfully to have the Senate's executive session debates published.[12] They could not have stood up in such numbers against a President of their own party, recently elected by a substantial majority, unless at least some of them expected public support.

Perhaps the antiannexationists counted on backing from taxpayers. Some, with former Democrats and former Whigs among their constituents, might have seen an advan-

[11] Fred Harvey Harrington, *Fighting Politician: Major General N. P. Banks* (Philadelphia, 1948), p. 186.

[12] *Journal of the Executive Proceedings of the Senate*, XVII, 407, 502–503.

tage in displaying independence of the administration. By and large, however, these legislators must have been looking for approval from the comparatively well-to-do, for it was this group which paid taxes and which from the beginning had misgivings about Grant, the tanner's son and onetime drunken ne'er-do-well. This group would also have been that most sensitive to currents in English and European thought.

Certainly the senators and representatives who led the fight against Grant's treaty had themselves felt the influence of liberal thought abroad. They were, by and large, the most cosmopolitan members of the two houses.

Sumner, a Harvard graduate of good family, had lived in Europe for two years and spoke several languages. He not only knew Bright but corresponded with him frequently and acted as host for friends of Bright who visited America.[13] An egotist who conceived of himself as a world-historical figure, Sumner believed with some reason that he enjoyed as high a standing among English as among American liberals. This fact may have had some direct bearing on his opposition to Dominican annexation, for at the time he saw his prestige among Englishmen as in jeopardy. He had recently spoken in the Senate about what Britain owed America on account of depredations by the British-built Confederate warship *Alabama*, suggesting that the British government cede Canada in compensation. Though partly

[13] Edward L. Pierce, *Memoir and Letters of Charles Sumner*, 4 vols. (London, 1898); "Bright-Sumner Letters, 1861–1872," *Proceedings of the Massachusetts Historical Society*, XLVI (1912–13), 93–164.

contrived to appease Irish and other Massachusetts voters who suspected their senator of Anglophilism, this proposition jibed with the views of Bright and others about the destiny of Canada. The form of it, however, vexed Sumner's English friends, and his standing with them plummeted. Conceivably Sumner hoped, by attacking Grant's Dominican scheme, to repair his reputation abroad. When he subsequently visited Bright in England he talked at length about his brave stand against colonialism.[14] But even if desire to please English liberals entered directly into Sumner's opposition to annexation, he need not have had Englishmen alone in mind, for he may have felt that being in tune with English liberalism counted for something with constituents at home. Liberal doctrine about colonies would thus have influenced Sumner, because he belonged to the international liberal community and also because elements in his public belonged to that community.

Of Schurz the same may be said. Already foremost among German-American politicians, he came from a well-to-do Rhenish family, had been a student at Bonn during the Revolution of 1848, had taken a prominent part in agitation for a liberal constitution, and had gone into exile when the Frankfurt experiment collapsed. Before emigrating to the United States he lived in Paris and London as part of a liberal fraternity that included not only other Germans but also Mazzini and Kossuth. In journalism and politics, first in Wisconsin and then in Missouri, Schurz benefited

[14] Walling, *Diaries of John Bright*, p. 351; Pierce, *Memoir and Letters of Charles Sumner*, IV, 543.

from a claim to be in the vanguard of international liberalism, and he made much use among German-American and other ethnic minorities of statements in his praise by famous foreigners. In opposing Grant's treaty Schurz assured himself of continued endorsements in the future.

In his speeches, however, Schurz addressed not foreign liberals but cosmopolitan Americans. He laid heavy stress on foreign experience. "England is growing wise with age," he said, "and English statesmen have before this day come to the conclusion that their old colonial system has ceased to be profitable, and whenever they can rid themselves of the colonies with honor, in most cases they will be very glad to do so." France was learning the same lesson, he went on, and Germany had developed the best colonial system in the world—"colonies not political, but colonies commercial." [15]

While we know less about other antiannexationists in the Senate, we know enough about a few to suggest that they too at least kept in touch with liberal thought abroad. The group included Lot M. Morrill of Maine, Joseph S. Fowler of Tennessee, and Thomas W. Tipton of Nebraska, all former college professors or presidents; William A. Buckingham of Connecticut and Waitman T. Willey of West Virginia, both men deeply concerned with Protestant foreign missions, and Buckingham also with the international temperance movement; and George F. Edmunds and Justin S. Morrill, both of Vermont, reputedly among the senators best versed in English political writing. The Democrats

[15] Bancroft, *Speeches and Papers of Carl Schurz*, II, 109–111.

who spoke most vehemently against annexation were Allen Thurman of Ohio, something of an authority on French literature, and Thomas F. Bayard of Delaware. By warning that annexation would "embark the government of the United States upon the vast and trackless sea of imperialism," Bayard displayed an understanding of the newest connotations of that new word.[16]

These senators evidently spoke for as well as to cosmopolitan Americans. Newspapers with large budgets of foreign news nearly all criticized Grant's treaty. Except for the New York *Herald*, none campaigned for annexation. Most of the Boston and Philadelphia press voiced outright opposition, as did the Springfield *Republican*, the *Nation*, and *Harper's Weekly*. The New York *Tribune* and even the New York *Times*, though then a slavish supporter of the Republican party, expressed doubts.[17] The former aboli-

[16] On Lot Morrill and Fowler, see *DAB*, XIII, 199, and VI, 564; on Buckingham, see Rev. Samuel G. Buckingham, *The Life of William A. Buckingham, the War Governor of Connecticut* (Springfield, Mass., 1894); on Willey, see Charles H. Ambler, *Waitman Thomas Willey* (Huntington, West Va., 1954); on Edmunds, *Biographical Encyclopedia of Vermont in the Nineteenth Century* (Boston, 1885), pp. 19–27; on Justin S. Morrill, *Memorial Addresses on The Life and Character of Justin S. Morrill* (Washington, D. C., 1899), esp. pp. 12, 18, 76, 86; on Thurman, *DAB*, XVIII, 515–516; on Bayard, *ibid.*, II, 70–72, and Charles Callan Tansill, *The Foreign Policy of Thomas F. Bayard, 1885–1897* (New York, 1940), pp. xi–xx. Bayard's speech is in 41 Cong., 3 sess., *Congressional Globe*, pp. 225–226.

[17] See Donald M. Dozer, "Anti-Expansionism during the Johnson Administration," *Pacific Historical Review*, XII (Sept. 1943), 253–275; Charles Callan Tansill, *United States and Santo Domingo, 1798–1873: A Chapter in Caribbean Diplomacy* (Baltimore, 1938), p. 433; Theodore Clark Smith, "Expansion after the Civil War, 1865–71," *Political Science Quarterly*, XVI, (Sept. 1901), 412–436.

tionist leaders, William Lloyd Garrison and Gerrit Smith, both friends of Bright and other English liberals, spoke out against annexation. So did Neal Dow, the temperance champion, who had similar ties. Among young Republicans openly endorsing the stand of Sumner and Schurz were Charles W. Eliot and E. L. Godkin.[18]

Two highly cosmopolitan men backed the President's plan—James Gordon Bennett, the publisher of the New York *Herald*, and Sam Ward.[19] Scottish-born and trained to be a Catholic priest, Bennett had begun his journalistic career translating Spanish-language news. He kept close watch on events in Latin America, traveled a good deal, and sent his son to Europe to be educated. Ward, the son of a New York banker, had graduated from Columbia University, lived for several years in Europe, and subsequently held diplomatic and quasi-diplomatic posts in Paraguay and Mexico. His close friends included William H. Russell, the American correspondent for the London *Times*, and Lord Rosebery. But both Bennett and Ward were mavericks. Bennett, who had sided with the South during the Civil

[18] On Garrison, see John L. Thomas, *The Liberator, William Lloyd Garrison, A Biography* (Boston, 1963), and Walter McIntosh Merrill, *Against Wind and Tide: A Biography of William Lloyd Garrison* (Cambridge, Mass., 1963); on Smith, see Ralph V. Harlow, *Gerrit Smith: Philanthropist and Reformer* (New York, 1939); on Dow, see his own *Reminiscences* (Portland, Me., 1898); see also William M. Armstrong, *E. L. Godkin and American Foreign Policy, 1865–1900* (New York, 1957), pp. 110–114.

[19] On Bennett, see *DAB*, II, 195–199; on Ward, see Maud Howe Elliott, *Uncle Sam Ward and His Circle* (New York, 1938), Louise Hall Tharp, *Three Saints and a Sinner: Julia Ward Howe, Louisa, Annie, and Sam Ward* (Boston, 1956), and Lately Thomas, *Sam Ward, King of the Lobby* (Boston, 1965).

War, voiced admiration for Louis Napoleon. Ward confessed his sympathies in English politics to lie with the Tories rather than the Liberals.[20] Moreover, Ward made his living as a lobbyist and a speculator, trading on inside political information, and probably had a stake in the Dominican concession.[21] On the whole, those Americans in touch with and in sympathy with liberal circles abroad adopted the anticolonial position fashionable in such circles.

These men were not necessarily slaves to foreign fashion. Shared experience and belief, mutual respect, and mutual deference made relations between Sumner, Schurz, Garrison, Smith, Dow, and their English friends somewhat like relations among opinion leaders within the United States. As Depew, Reid, and Holls would later consult one another to make sure that Republicans had a common position, so American, English, and German liberals consulted one another to ensure liberal unity. As members of an international community, American liberals felt the effects of currents within that community, just as they felt the effects, as Americans, of their nation's peculiar historical traditions and economic requirements.

These elements probably cannot be disentangled. Sumner and Schurz may have judged the American past by standards of liberalism, seeing extension of suffrage and improvement of public morality as far more important than

[20] The Marquess of Crewe, *Lord Rosebery*, 2 vols. (London, 1931), I, 67–68, 95–96.

[21] Elliott, *Uncle Sam Ward*, pp. 494–499, tells of his interest in the Dominican issue; Thomas, *Sam Ward*, pp. 303–4, 312–313, 341–342, 350, 354 and 356, describes his close connections with Samuel Barlow, a New York merchant much involved in Dominican speculation.

increases in territory or national power. Similarly, they may have calculated economic interest by liberal criteria, setting a higher value on manufacturing and trade than on land and agriculture, assuming that governmental action usually impeded economic progress, and accepting as dogma the worthlessness of colonies. At the same time, owing to awareness of their country's distinctive past and economic conditions, they held their own varieties of liberal belief— as, in the most obvious example, regarding free trade as wise for England but not for the United States. Cosmopolitan Americans felt the same influences as other Americans, but felt in addition influences that touched more lightly fellow countrymen of more limited horizon.

Some citizens in the latter category sensed the difference and resented it. In the Dominican debate proannexationists attacked their opponents as Europeanized and insufficiently "American." Conkling and Nye ridiculed Sumner's French pronunciation of the term "aide-de-camp," and Democratic Senator John W. Stevenson of Kentucky called for taking the Dominican Republic on account of "our boasted doctrine of American independence of Europe." Looking back later, the Chicago *Tribune* explained the opposition of the New York press to expansion by asserting, "New York faces east and not west . . . it thinks more of what is going on across the Atlantic than of what happens on this side of the Alleghenies." [22]

While cosmopolitan types probably bulked large in the

[22] 41 Cong., 3 sess., *Congressional Globe*, pp. 240, 245, 410; Philip Kinsley, *The Chicago Tribune, Its First Hundred Years*, 3 vols. (Chicago, 1945–1946), III, 145.

foreign policy public and certainly did so in the establishment, some members of this public evidently had a bias against cosmopolitanism, holding that Americans ought not to be influenced by European thought or experience. On the evidence of the Dominican debate, this anticosmopolitan element would seem to have consisted of the less educated and less prosperous who, for one reason or another, took interest in a foreign policy issue. And in 1869–71 experienced politicians—for example, Banks, Conkling, Morton, and Orth—bet on arousing enough such citizens to constitute an effective public.

These politicians proved to be wrong. The evidence that accumulated in Washington showed opinion to be against Dominican annexation. The junior senator from Massachusetts stood by Grant; but he confessed that interested voters in his state were probably nine-to-one against annexation. Justice Jacob Brinkerhoff of the Ohio Supreme Court estimated that not a thousand people in the whole country enthusiastically backed the President's plan, and the Indiana legislature passed a resolution condemning Morton for supporting it.[23]

Men of the establishment and elements of the public affiliated with them united on a single opinion. Seeing this trend, the administration attempted to divide the establishment. For a proannexation rally in New York's Cooper Union, Grant tried to enlist as chairman his good friend John A. Dix, a polished, well-traveled, and well-to-do busi-

[23] Pierce, *Memoir and Letters of Charles Sumner*, IV, 442; Tansill, *United States and Santo Domingo*, p. 433, n. 87; William Dudley Foulke, *Life of Oliver P. Morton*, 2 vols. (Indianapolis, 1899), II, 168, n. 1.

nessman who had just returned from three years as United States Minister to France. Dix refused, however. So did others. The administration had to fall back on Moses Grinnell, who, though head of a shipping firm, a frequent transatlantic traveler, and a onetime figure in the antislavery movement, held the patronage post of Collector of the Port of New York. Even Bennett's *Herald* had to report the rally as merely a turnout of placemen.[24]

After the treaty's defeat in the Senate Grant prevailed on Congress to authorize appointment of a commission to report on conditions in the Dominican Republic, hoping thus to prompt reconsideration. To this commission the administration appointed two men with establishment credentials: Andrew D. White, the learned and much traveled thirty-eight-year-old president of Cornell University, and Samuel Gridley Howe, a veteran reformer who had not only been prominent as an abolitionist but had championed Greek independence in the 1820s and, most recently, led agitation in behalf of Cretans seeking freedom from Turkish rule. After a refusal from forty-eighter Franz Sigel, the third place went to Senator Benjamin F. Wade of Ohio, whose only obvious qualification was a reputation for bluff honesty.[25]

As a maneuver to break the ranks of the establishment,

[24] Tansill, *United States and Santo Domingo*, p. 408; on Dix see Morgan Dix, comp., *Memoirs of John Adams Dix*, 2 vols. (New York, 1883); *New York Herald*, May 13, 1870.

[25] Andrew Dickson White, *Autobiography*, 2 vols. (New York, 1905), I, 181, 483–507; Harold Schwartz, *Samuel Gridley Howe, Social Reformer, 1801–1876* (Cambridge, Mass., 1956), pp. 281, 291–297; Tansill, *United States and Santo Domingo*, p. 436, n. 98; H. L. Trefousse, *Benjamin Franklin Wade, Radical Republican from Ohio* (New York, 1963), pp. 313–315, 372.

the appointment of this commission failed. Describing optimistically the Dominican Republic's prospects for political and economic progress, its report provided data useful to Grant's supporters, but White, the most cosmopolitan of the trio, refused to endorse a recommendation for annexation. Though Howe did so, his stand could be marked down to his yearning for appointment as Minister to Greece and the fact that he was Sam Ward's brother-in-law. The commission report had no apparent impact on effective public opinion, and the whole annexation scheme died a quiet death.

During succeeding decades this episode became one of the precedents by which Americans guided themselves. Indeed, it became a key precedent. In 1869–71 history had seemed on the side of the expansionists. The Dominican decision gave the nation a new interpretation of its past, for Americans saw their forebears as having chosen to conquer a continent but not to go beyond the sea's edge or into the tropics. Those arguing later for a different policy had to contend against belief in a national anti-imperialist tradition. The episode thus had what an economist might call a multiplier effect.

In the Dominican case we see the influence on American thought of currents running within a larger Atlantic community. We also see this influence contributing to differences in opinion between cosmopolitan and insular Americans—differences all the wider because lines between the two groups coincided with economic and social divisions. Since cosmopolites inevitably formed a disproportionate part of the foreign policy public, their unity in this instance meant that their opinion registered with politicians as public opinion. Before turning to the debates of the 1890s we need to review developments of the intervening years that affected the views of cosmopolitan Americans.

VI

NEW TURNS IN THOUGHT

Anticolonialism remained a vigorous liberal doctrine throughout the century. Goldwin Smith continued to write in the vein of *The Empire*. By leaving Oxford for Cornell and living thereafter in either the United States or Canada, he added to his American following. John Bright survived until the end of the 1880s, with his opposition to imperialism never waning and his circle of American admirers growing larger as the years passed.

William Ewart Gladstone meanwhile began to rival Bright as an American hero. During the Civil War he had not been conspicuously pro-Union. Indeed, he outraged Union patriots by calling the Confederacy a nation. As Prime Minister in the later sixties, however, he agreed to an openhanded settlement of the *Alabama* claims. In words that were to be quoted (or more often paraphrased) in thousands of American orations he characterized the U. S.

Constitution as "the most remarkable work known to me in modern times to have been produced by the human intellect, at a single stroke (so to speak), in its application to political affairs." In office or on the opposition front bench he preached the purest Protestant morality, declaring that England and all Christian states should put freedom, right, and justice ahead of any selfish national interest. Toward the end of an almost interminable career he turned into a champion of home rule for Ireland, thus asking for the righting of what nearly all Americans regarded as a wrong and, in addition, offering hope that the Irish would be deprived of the cause which united them as a political bloc in the United States. So much admired was Gladstone that his death in 1898 produced a page or more of obituary in most leading American dailies and memorial sermons in hundreds of American churches. And all the while Gladstone spoke for anticolonialism.

Though no later English or European liberal had a following in America equal to Bright's or Gladstone's, two younger English liberals, James Bryce and John Morley, gained great popularity among Americans.[1] A former pupil of Goldwin Smith's and Regius Professor of Civil Law at Oxford, Bryce made his first visit to the United States in 1870. Modest, interested in many subjects, and a good listener, he charmed New England littérateurs and became friendly with, among others, Eliot and Godkin. Entering Parliament four years later as an ardent Gladstonian, he be-

[1] See H. A. L. Fisher, *James Bryce*, 2 vols. (New York, 1927), and James, Viscount Morley, *Recollections*, 2 vols. (New York, 1917).

117

came a more and more prominent figure in his homeland. Meanwhile he maintained ties with Americans by contributing to the New York *Nation* and serving as host for visitors from the United States. In the early 1880s he began the extensive travel in America that was to result in *The American Commonwealth*. Four-fifths of that book, he said later, drew upon conversations with such friends as Eliot, Lodge, Godkin, Low, Seligman, Theodore Roosevelt, Andrew D. White, and John Hay.[2] Mirroring faithfully the views of these men on both the strengths and the shortcomings of American democracy, his work naturally won their acclaim. Probably the Englishman, after Bright and Gladstone, best known and most respected in the United States, Bryce lent all his prestige to the traditional liberal doctrine regarding colonies.

Morley owed his standing in America to reflection from Gladstone's light. Though an agnostic, he seemed more nearly a politician of conscience than any Liberal except the Grand Old Man himself, and on the Irish question he stood a step ahead of his leader. Having toured the United States in the late sixties, he had gathered a circle of American acquaintances similar to Bryce's. With Andrew Carnegie he established a close friendship, and though he did not cross the Atlantic again until 1904, he passed many weekends with Americans visiting Carnegie at Skibo Castle.[3] For all of these and for others who knew him only by repute,

[2] Fisher, *James Bryce*, I, 238; James Bryce, *The American Commonwealth*, 3rd ed., 2 vols. (New York, 1894), I, vii–xi.

[3] Burton J. Hendrick, *The Life and Letters of Andrew Carnegie*, 2 vols. (Garden City, N. Y., 1932), I, 238, II, 178–179.

Morley, like Bryce, represented a younger generation (both turned sixty in 1898) holding steadfastly to the anti-colonial faith.

Meanwhile, however, a new strain of liberal thought budded. It could be dimly glimpsed as early as 1869 in a book published in both London and New York, Charles Wentworth Dilke's *Greater Britain*.[4]

For Americans, Dilke's book made as gratifying reading as any of Bright's or Gladstone's speeches. Though widely sold in England, it had more buyers in the United States than at home, probably because it said so much that Americans wanted to believe. *Greater Britain* called the Union's victory "the noblest blow for freedom that the world has seen"; it said the postwar Negro problem would vanish as Negroes, freed from slavery, proved unable to compete with superior races and melted away like the Maoris and the American Indians; and it predicted that Americans of Anglo-Saxon background would absorb or master Irish, German, and other immigrant groups. At total variance with Bright, Dilke defended the Republican policy of establishing protective tariffs. Tariffs, Dilke wrote, were symbols of American idealism; they were "not supported by a selfish clique, but rest upon the generosity and self-sacrifice of a majority of the population," for they shielded the Anglo-Saxon strongholds of the interior and allowed the West to

---

[4] Charles Wentworth Dilke, *Greater Britain: A Record of Travel in English-Speaking Countries During 1866 and 1867* (New York, 1869). Quoted passages are from pp. 53, 328, ix, 491, 546, 198, 546. See C. A. Bodelson, *Studies in Mid-Victorian Imperialism* (Copenhagen, 1924), pp. 60–76.

resist domination by port cities where Irish were in control.

Regarding colonies, Dilke wrote as an orthodox liberal. He spoke of the burden, expense, and danger they entailed and described possession of Canada by Britain rather than the United States as "opposed to the best interests of our race." Nevertheless *Greater Britain* had a tone never present in Bright's speeches. Through it ran pride in the vastness of the empire and a half-voiced belief that Anglo-Saxons, as the foremost among races, might be the predestined masters of the earth. Dilke referred to "the grandeur of our race, already girdling the earth, which it is destined, perhaps, eventually to overspread." With regard to India, he could not help saying that English "rule means the moral advancement of their country" and he stated further:

> The possession of India offers to ourselves that element of vastness of dominion which, in this age, is needed to secure width of thought and nobility of purpose; but to the English race our possession of India, of the coasts of Africa, and of the ports of China offers the possibility of planting free institutions among the dark-skinned races of the world.

Though an immature twenty-seven when the book appeared, Dilke already held a seat in Parliament and promised soon to be a commanding figure in the Liberal party. The rest of what he wrote had so much appeal for Americans as perhaps to make palatable his attitude toward empire, especially since he coupled Americans with Englishmen in all he said. In the Orient, declared Dilke, "the future has no bounds: through California and the Sandwich Islands, through Japan, fast becoming American, and China, the coast of which is already British, our race seems marching westward to universal rule." His final page even invited Americans to lead the march: "The ultimate future of any one section of our race . . . is of little moment by the side of its triumph as a whole, but the power of English laws and English principles of government is not merely an English question—its continuance is essential to the freedom of mankind."

Conceivably the view of empire in *Greater Britain* reflected Dilke's extensive travel in the United States. At the time of Dilke's American tour Seward was in the State Department; the United States had just added Alaska to its domains; and the Danish West Indies and the Dominican Republic seemed on the verge of becoming American. Some sense of the Manifest Destiny tradition may have reached Dilke and may have affected his vision of what lay in store for all Anglo-Saxons. If so, then *Greater Britain* protected a germ of that tradition from the change of 1869–71. For nearly twenty years Dilke remained a rising star in English politics. Before a divorce scandal destroyed his career he reached the Cabinet, with gossip naming him as a future Premier, and during all that time *Greater Britain* remained in print and continued to be bought, read, and quoted by Americans.[5]

Other books, articles, and speeches circulating in the

[5] Stephen Gwynn and Gertrude M. Tuckwell, *The Life of the Rt. Hon. Sir Charles W. Dilke*, 2 vols. (London, 1917), I, 69; Roy Jenkins, *Sir Charles Dilke, A Victorian Tragedy* (London, 1965), pp. 42, 372; Preface to Dilke, *Problems of Greater Britain* (London, 1890).

1870s jarred even more than Dilke's with the orthodox view of colonies. Paul Leroy-Beaulieu's *De la colonisation chez les peuples modernes*, published in Paris in 1874 and quickly read throughout Europe, accepted the standard liberal arguments but contended that they applied only to such colonies as those of Britain in North America, peopled by settlers from a mother country.[6] If advanced nations took control of areas already populated by backward peoples, Leroy-Beaulieu reasoned, everyone benefited. The advanced nations obtained markets for their products and outlets for their capital, and backward natives gained not only opportunities for economic progress but also stimulating contact with superior cultures. Mercantilism being passé, Leroy-Beaulieu argued, colonies would eventually offer trade and investment opportunities for other nations, to the gain of the whole world.

Leroy-Beaulieu's fame grew. Thirty-one in 1874, he reached at thirty-six the peak of academic recognition, becoming a professor at the Collège de France. His ideas, discussed throughout Europe, reached Americans visiting or studying with European scholars. American periodicals reviewed or summarized Leroy-Beaulieu's later studies. In 1896 the Republican party distributed an English translation of a pamphlet by him championing the gold standard.[7]

[6] Paul Leroy-Beaulieu, *De la colonisation chez les peuples modernes* (Paris, 1874). An extensive analysis of Leroy-Beaulieu's thought appears in Agnes Murphy, *The Ideology of French Imperialism, 1871–1881* (Washington, D. C., 1948). See also Henri Brunschwig, *French Colonialism, 1871–1914: Myths and Realities* (London, 1966), pp. 26–28.

[7] Paul Leroy-Beaulieu, *Silver, Yesterday and Today: The Case Against Bimetallism* (Boston, 1896).

Like *Greater Britain*, *La colonisation chez les peuples modernes* conceivably encouraged Americans to take a less dim view of the value of colonies.

From Germany too came challenges to the orthodoxy of mid-century. Faith in free trade, never as strong in Germany as in Britain or France, grew weaker during the prolonged agricultural and economic depression of the 1870s. At the end of the decade, as Bryce's imaginary businessman read in his morning paper, Bismarck initiated a protective policy. Meanwhile concern mounted about the outflow of emigrants to the United States, and several writers produced pamphlets and books urging development of overseas colonies.

Friedrich Fabri, the most important of these authors, brought out his book *Bedarf Deutschland der Colonien?* (Does Germany Need Colonies?) in 1879.[8] An official of a Catholic missionary organization in the Rhineland, Fabri had become interested in the subject as a result of visiting missions in Africa and Latin America. In his book, however, he minimized moral and religious aspects of the question. His emphasis went instead to the economic and political needs of the German state.

While Britain, France, Russia, and the United States all owned empty lands, Fabri said, Germany, the nation "most expansive, fastest growing, and most capable of developing

[8] Friedrich Fabri, *Bedarf Deutschland der Colonien? Eine politisch-ökonomische Betrachtung*, 3rd ed. (Gotha, 1884). Quotations are from pp. 22–24 and 77. The background of German colonialist thought is best sketched in Mack Walker, *Germany and the Emigration, 1816–1885* (Cambridge, Mass., 1964), pp. 199–239.

colonies (*colonial-befähig*)," had none. Emigration to foreign countries cost Germany labor worth 300 million marks a year, the total loss as of 1879 coming to 15 billion marks. Even so, the country remained overpopulated, with resultant harm to its economy.

Partly because Fabri's economic logic differs so from that which relates colonialism to excess productive capacity, his argument deserves quotation. He wrote:

> It is said that overpopulation begins when importation of necessary foodstuffs exceeds their exportation. Certainly this is true, but it is not sufficient as a definition. A nation can be compelled to import huge quantities of foodstuffs without the natural effects of the onset of overpopulation asserting themselves. If output and sale of industrial products are sufficiently large and stable that it can not only easily bear food imports but protect its purchasing and saving power, its national prosperity can grow. This has been in fact the case with England. . . . If, however, industrial production declines and employment and earnings fall off, then the calamitous nature of overpopulation becomes ever more apparent, and want and poverty rapidly spread; then the generally accepted view of the effect of population growth on national prosperity is proven to have only limited validity. The point of this for the present situation of Germany is self-evident. Our agricultural pro-

duction supplies from year to year less of our needs, and our industrial production has been in unprecedented decline for years and is now at a deep low. A perceptible increase in agricultural production can develop only slowly and within narrow limits—much too slowly to catch up in any way with the growing overpopulation. And our industry must also be inadequate. Even assuming that in a decade . . . it will again reach such a level that it can again employ as many people as in 1873 . . . there will be in a decade from now so-and-so many million people more in Germany to feed, clothe, and instruct.

Fabri argued that overpopulation had other effects. It put strains on the schools and thus affected the quality of education. Given the principle of universal military service, it caused the army to be bigger and hence more expensive. Worst of all, by contributing to discontent, it promoted the growth of socialism. All these ills could be remedied, he believed, by a colonial empire.

Fabri recommended acquisition of two kinds of colonies, agricultural and commercial. The first could not only take care of excess population but also increase the supply of food. The second would bring German industry a flow of nonagricultural raw materials.

As sites for agricultural colonies Fabri pointed to the nontropical parts of South America—the Brazilian province of Rio Grande do Sul and countries of the Plata basin.

Held as protectorates until Germans became a majority, these areas would eventually serve Germany as Canada, Australia, and New Zealand served Britain. As sites for commercial colonies Fabri singled out sections of the African coast and Samoa and other islands in the Pacific.

"Has Germany a . . . right to follow the indicated course?" he asked rhetorically, replying:

> It would be hard for anyone to answer this question in the negative. Indeed, one can go farther and say: in view of emigration resulting from growing overpopulation, in view of the evident general economic situation, Germany already finds herself at a crossroads where she is required, as a necessity of life . . . to move in this direction. The colonial question shows itself more and more as a question of existence, and it is the right and duty of any state to pursue the necessities of life with all the resources it can command and, if necessary, also with its power.

Fabri's themes appeared in most later German writings and speeches in favor of colonies: the nation lost from emigration to foreign countries; emigration nevertheless had to occur because of overpopulation; colonies permitted emigration without loss and, in addition, gave the mother country access to new supplies of food and raw materials; since other nations had empires, right, duty, and need combined to require that Germany have one too.

Known to at least some Americans, Fabri had been one of

a handful of prominent Germans brought to the United States by Villard to celebrate the opening of the Northern Pacific Railroad. The German-American press not only reviewed his works but alluded to them as if their contents were common knowledge.[9]

The writings of Fabri and other German colonialists did not, however, hold much appeal for German-Americans. By implication they condemned past German emigration as unpatriotic. If the German government accepted their reasoning, it would halt the flow of Germans to America and hence frustrate German-American hopes of becoming a larger force in their adopted country. Since America had vacant land and factories running at less than capacity, the economic arguments of German colonialists made less sense to German-American than to German readers.

Fabri and his counterparts probably made few converts in the United States. Those German-American leaders who swung toward imperialism in the 1890s had more admiration for English than for German thought. Holls, as an example, remained critical of German colonial ambitions at the same time that he endorsed American annexation of the Philippines.[10] For most German-Americans, acquaintance with German imperialist literature would, if anything, have fortified rather than weakened anticolonial beliefs.

[9] Alfred Vagts, *Deutschland und die Vereinigten Staaten in der Weltpolitik*, 2 vols. (New York, 1935), I, 433; Henry Villard, *Memoirs*, 2 vols. (Boston, 1904), II, 315. Listing Fabri among Villard's guests, the *New Yorker Staatszeitung*, Oct. 2, 1883, described him as "the well known author," though *Bedarf Deutschland der Colonien?* was his only work as of that date.

[10] Vagts, *Deutschland und die Vereinigten Staaten*, I, 578, 583.

The chief current running counter to the traditional liberal view of colonies came therefore from England. Leroy-Beaulieu sounded the proper notes—destiny, duty to backward peoples, and benefit to mankind; but he had the Gallic failing of excessive precision. In his later writings he distinguished one class of desirable possessions as "colonies for exploitation." Other French colonialists confessed even more frankly that natives would benefit only as they worked their way up from the status of slave labor. In Dilke's formulation, natives either prospered or disappeared.

Two important English works of the 1880s developed the ideas that Dilke had tentatively set forth: Sir John Seeley's *The Expansion of England* and James Anthony Froude's *Oceana*.[11]

The renown of Seeley, a professor of classics at Cambridge, rested on *Ecce Homo*, a historical but not impious account of the life of Jesus. *The Expansion of England* grew from a set of public lectures on a subject obviously outside Seeley's specialty. A thin, readable volume, it attacked what Seeley described as the prevailing feeling that England had had her day—that, having led the world toward freedom, representative government, and economic progress, she now faced outstripping by nations following

11 J. R. Seeley, *The Expansion of England* (Boston, 1883); James Anthony Froude, *Oceana or England and Her Colonies* (New York, 1886). Quotations from Seeley are from pp. 155, 168, 196. On Seeley, see Bodelson, *Mid-Victorian Imperialism*, pp. 149–175, and Harry A. Gailey, Jr., "Seeley and the Expansion of England," *Northwest Missouri State College Studies*, Vol. XXIV, No. 2 (1959).

her footsteps. Such a view resulted from an unnecessarily narrow angle of vision, Seeley contended, for if one looked beyond the Channel and the Irish Sea, he would observe that the great current of recent history, only beginning to run, involved the spread of Englishmen and English institutions to the farthest parts of the earth.

In many respects a traditionalist and a Gladstonian, Seeley frowned on the term "empire." Like Dilke, he stressed the virtues of voluntary association and praised the American model. "I suppose," wrote Seeley, "there has never been in any community so much happiness, or happiness of a kind so little demoralising, as in the United States." The causes he cited as: "Characters formed in a temperate zone, by Teutonic liberty and Protestant religion; prosperity conferred freely but in measure, and on the condition not only of labour but of the use of intelligence and ingenuity." Seeley stated as the great question of the future, "Will the English race, which is divided by so many oceans . . . devise some organisation like that of the United States, under which full liberty and solid union may be reconciled with unbounded territorial extension?"

As to India, Seeley voiced two opinions. On the one hand, he described it as an expensive, onerous, and dangerous possession. On the other hand, like Dilke, he saw continuation of British rule as necessary. To abandon the subcontinent would bring an end to Indian progress and leave the Indians at the mercy of Russia and, he said roundly, "would be the most inexcusable of all conceivable crimes and might possibly cause the most stupendous of all conceivable calamities."

Using stronger words than Dilke, Seeley came nearer to a position that could be called imperialist, but did so from points of departure in liberal anticolonial orthodoxy. This fact, coupled with evident admiration for the United States, made Seeley's message acceptable to Americans still strongly of Bright's persuasion. Godkin, for example, praised *The Expansion of England* as "singularly thoughtful and suggestive." [12]

Froude's *Oceana* did not appear until 1886. In the meantime the reach into America of ideas such as those of Dilke and Seeley had been evidenced by John Fiske's "Manifest Destiny" lecture.[13] Prepared for an English audience and first delivered in London, this lecture described the spread of English ideas and institutions and predicted their ultimate conquest of the entire earth. Even the final version, published in 1886 after being heard by hundreds of American audiences, said nothing about American expansion or, indeed, about the expansion of any nation's holdings. Fiske's prophecies had to do solely with men's minds.

Froude went well beyond either Dilke, Seeley, or Fiske.[14]

[12] *Nation*, XXXVII (Dec. 6, 1883), 473.

[13] John Fiske, *American Political Ideas Viewed from the Standpoint of Universal History* (New York, 1885), pp. 101–152; Milton Berman, *John Fiske* (Cambridge, Mass., 1961), writes: "the belief that the entire evolution of the world had purposefully prepared for the rise of New England, and that the future world would see the spread of its ideas all over the globe—this was the basic concept that informed all Fiske's historical writing" (p. 268).

[14] Quotations from Froude, *Oceana*, are from pp. 345, 354, 13, 388. On Froude, see Bodelson, *Mid-Victorian Imperialism*, pp. 176–204; Harry A. Gailey, Jr., "James Anthony Froude and the Colonial Question," *North-*

He showed traces of traditional liberal views on colonies only in stray passages lamenting civilization's effects on noble savages (as, for example, one describing Hawaiian natives as "innocent, and happy, and prosperous before the white man and his 'notions' came among them"). More often Froude evidenced an unquestioning belief in the superiority of English culture. He voiced doubt about its eventual overwhelming of all others solely because he questioned whether English-speaking people would stand together and show the fortitude to do what needed doing.

On the first point Froude, like earlier writers, paid respects to the United States. "The problem of how to combine a number of self-governed communities into a single commonwealth," he wrote, ". . . has been solved, and solved completely, in the American union." Froude advocated an effort by Britain and her colonies to achieve a comparable union.

On the second point Froude went beyond his predecessors. He characterized control not only of India but of all "lower civilizations" as desirable. Disputing the calculations of mid-century liberals, Froude claimed that India had returned a handsome profit. Other colonies would pay like returns, he declared, for "commerce follows the flag."

But Froude saw economic benefit as only one return from colonies and by no means the most important, for colonies would enable English-speaking peoples to carry out

west Missouri State College Studies, Vol. XXI, No. 3 (1957); and Waldo Hilary Dunn, James Anthony Froude, A Biography, 2 vols. (Oxford, 1963).

their great mission of spreading Christianity, representative institutions, and the rule of law. He wrote that "in theological language, it is the saving of our national soul, it is the saving of the souls of millions of Englishmen hereafter to be born, that is really at stake; and once more the old choice is again before us, whether we prefer immediate money advantage . . . or else our spiritual salvation." If men who spoke English did not take up the challenge, Froude asserted, they would fall behind in the international struggle for existence.

That Froude's words would not have been startling to all Americans is evident in the Reverend Josiah Strong's *Our Country*, published in the same year.[15] The work of a clergyman who had never lived east of the Alleghenies, it appeared under the imprint of the Congregationalist Home Missionary Society. Most of its chapters attacked Romanism, Mormonism, intemperance, socialism, excessive wealth, cities, and other "perils" to be fought by upright conduct and donations to the Missionary Society. But one chapter, subsequently famed, dealt with the destiny of Anglo-Saxons to be the earth's rulers. While assigning England and her colonies a role in this destiny, it placed Americans in the forefront. It forecast, as the accomplishment of

15 The best version is the John Harvard Library edition, reprinting the edition of 1891, with an Introduction by Jurgen Herbst (Cambridge, Mass., 1963). Dorothea R. Muller, "Josiah Strong and American Nationalism: A Reevaluation," *Journal of American History*, LIII (Dec. 1966), 487–503, shows that passages in Strong seeming to plead for physical conquest of underdeveloped areas were neither so intended nor so read. What was understood was moral conquest very similar to what Fiske advocated.

God's will, conquest for Anglo-Saxondom of Latin America, the Pacific area, and Africa. That 130,000 copies of *Our Country* could appear within five years without the book's exciting protest indicates that by the mid-1880s the language of expansionism already had some new currency in America.[16]

For the moment Froude's *Oceana* probably had greater influence within the foreign policy public. A noted scholar and author of multivolume histories of Tudor England and the English in Ireland, Froude had lectured in America in the early 1870s. As a result of being harassed by Irish nationalists he became a hero among anti-Irish Americans. His reputation having grown in the meantime, he received a clamorous reception when he revisited the United States in 1885. As author of an official report on south Africa, he appeared to have special qualifications for writing about colonies, and the fact that his report recommended relaxation of colonial rule enhanced the effect of his new message.[17] Americans of the establishment would have regarded Froude with respect, and *Oceana*, even more than Dilke's and Seeley's books, could have caused those steeped in the anticolonial tradition to question that tradition.

If Strong's book had a similar effect, it probably came later. After publication of *Our Country* the English-based Evangelical Alliance employed Strong as General Secretary for its American branch. Chapters of his book were ex-

[16] *Our Country* (John Harvard Library edition), p. 3.
[17] See James Anthony Froude, *Two Lectures on South Africa*, new ed. (London, 1900).

133

cerpted and published in England as *The United States and the Future of the Anglo-Saxon Race*. In 1891, when a revised edition of *Our Country* appeared, it had a cachet lacking in 1886.

Meanwhile another work by an American had come out, Captain Mahan's celebrated *Influence of Sea Power on History*. Greeted with acclaim in England, it immediately had a good press in the United States—the more so as time passed and England's political aristocracy lionized Mahan.[18]

Mahan, of course, emphasized maritime power. From England's rise in the seventeenth and eighteenth centuries he deduced that ships, naval bases, and colonies were the keys to greatness. A people wishing to progress and to carry out the mission Froude described had better, Mahan advised, ensure themselves of ironclads and coaling stations. In subsequent magazine articles he stressed that this rule applied to Americans no less than to others.

Instead of occasional works questioning the anticolonial gospel, the decade after 1890 saw an outpouring of books, articles, and pamphlets advertising the positive virtues of colonies.[19] Lord Curzon's *Problems of the Far East* pictured

[18] Charles Carlisle Taylor, *The Life of Admiral Mahan* (London, 1920), pp. 46, 61–63; W. D. Puleston, *Mahan* (New Haven, 1934), pp. 135, 141, 156; William E. Livezey, *Mahan on Sea Power* (Norman, Okla., 1947), pp. 51–92.

[19] The best summary of European colonial fervor in the 1890s is still to be found in William L. Langer, *The Diplomacy of Imperialism*, 2nd ed. (New York, 1950), pp. 67–96; but see also Georg W. F. Hallgarten, *Imperialismus vor 1914: die soziologischen Grundlagen der Aussenpolitik europäischer Grossmächte vor dem ersten Weltkrieg*, rev. ed., 2 vols. (Munich, 1963), I, *passim*, and A. P. Thornton, *Doctrines of Imperialism* (New York, 1965). Friedrich Brie, *Imperialistische Strömungen in der*

as yet unexploited opportunities for carrying on England's civilizing mission. Alfred Milner's *England in Egypt* glorified what had been accomplished on the Nile.[20] Much literature came from organizations: in Germany, a Colonial Society, made up of parliamentary leaders and industrialists mostly from western Germany, and a Pan German League, which enlisted many politicians and intellectuals and took a more chauvinistic line; in France, a Committee for French Africa and a French Colonial Union, consisting of geographers and other scholars, representatives of banks and import-export houses, army and navy officers, and politicians from the republican right; in England, the Primrose League and the Imperial Federation League.[21] Neither Curzon's work nor Milner's nor the vast pamphlet output of procolonial organizations said much that had not been said by Dilke, Leroy-Beaulieu, Fabri, Seeley, Froude, or Mahan.

Charles Henry Pearson's *National Life and Character* represented the only new line of imperialist thought to mature in the nineties.[22] In it Pearson pictured European races

---

englischen Literatur, 2nd enlarged ed. (Halle, 1928), suggests the extent to which imperialism permeated English literature, but see also Bodelson, *Mid-Victorian Imperialism,* pp. 22–32, 124–132, who voices reservations on this point.

[20] George Nathaniel Curzon, *Problems of the Far East: Japan, Corea, China* (London, 1894); Alfred Milner, *England in Egypt* (London, 1893). See reviews in the *Nation,* LVI (March 23, 1893), 218–219, and LIX (Oct. 4, 1894), 250–251.

[21] See Brunschwig, *French Colonialism,* pp. 105–134, Jacques Chastenet, *Histoire de la troisième république,* 4 vols. (Paris, 1952–56), II, 165–278, and Hallgarten, *Imperialismus vor 1914,* I, 100–104.

[22] Charles H. Pearson, *National Life and Character, a Forecast* (New York, 1893). Quotations below are from pp. 152, 13–14, 85. On Pearson, see the biographical sketch by Herbert A. Strong in Charles H. Pearson,

as imprisoned in temperate zones rapidly becoming over-populated. Increasingly crowded together in cities, Pearson believed they were sure to "lose stamina, and decline in stature, to a degree that implies perilous degeneracy." Considering their needs, the narrow and selfish outlook encouraged by city life, and the power the urban masses would possess, Pearson saw a trend toward "State Socialism" as inevitable; and he did not except the United States, which he viewed as nearing its capacity in population and already on the road to statism. Life in future days, Pearson prophesied, would be materially more comfortable and freer from disease, but humdrum, regimented, and uncreative; and some day the lesser, darker races, with larger breeding grounds, would come out of the tropics to overwhelm Aryan civilization.

Pearson saw little hope. While conceding that future history might hold some surprises, he expressed doubt that overpopulation, urbanization, degeneration, or State Socialism could be averted. His counsel was to acknowledge the likelihood of the worst but to do what might be done to ameliorate it. Specifically he recommended continuing to test whether or not the tropics were habitable by Europeans, adding "if we cannot change manifest destiny, we may at least adapt ourselves to it, and make it endurable. We may circumscribe the growth of China, though we cannot altogether arrest it; and if we cannot hope that Europeans will ever people Africa, we may at least so work

Reviews and Critical Essays (London, 1896), pp. 1–38, and William Stebbing, _Charles Henry Pearson_ (London, 1900).

that European ideas shall one day be paramount from the Red Sea to the Atlantic." Even if defeated, Pearson observed, Europeans could say to themselves, "It has been our work to organize and create, to carry peace and law and order over the world, that others may enter in and enjoy."

Benjamin Kidd's *Social Evolution* paralleled Pearson's work but stated a more complex case.[23] While also foreseeing degeneration in society and increase in state power, Kidd believed he saw "*a tendency to strengthen and equip at the general expense the lower and weaker against the higher and wealthier classes of the community*" (Kidd's italics) and also a tendency toward "the general abandonment of the doctrine of the noninterference of the state in social matters." Kidd argued that study of history showed the interests of a race or nation seldom to have been the same as the interests of the individuals composing it. Like soldiers in an army, individuals suffered so that the common enterprise could succeed. The observable tendencies toward social equality and state power offered hope, in Kidd's view, that the interests of the collectivity and its members would come closer together.

The danger Kidd saw lay not in the trends themselves but in the possibility of their gathering runaway speed. Greater social equality and greater state power held no ter-

[23] Benjamin Kidd, *Social Evolution* (New York, 1894). Quotations are from pp. 219, 255, 282, 340, 308. See Bernard Semmel, *Imperialism and Social Reform: English Social-Imperial Thought, 1895–1914* (London, 1960), pp. 31–35. Semmel emphasizes the roles of Kidd and Karl Pearson in formulating the ideology of "External Social-Darwinism." He does not deal with Charles Henry Pearson.

ror for him so long as the state merely assumed *"functions in order to preserve or secure free competition"* (Kidd's italics). Socialism, however, would mean the doom of competition and hence, in his view, the end of all progress. Without competition, he believed, all standards would descend toward those of the lowest classes, whose numbers were "accumulating on the principle of compound interest."

In a long discussion of colonial opportunities Kidd implied that the solution lay in overseas expansion. Like Pearson, he regarded the tropics as unsuitable for white colonization, but he held that, with their growing numbers and needs, whites could not allow the resources of the tropics to be wasted much longer. Hence, he predicted, "the European races will gradually come to realise that the tropics must be administered from the temperate regions."

Also, Kidd suggested, enterprise in the tropics might encourage precisely the right kind of character evolution, for he viewed brain power as only partially fitting man for survival and success. He wrote:

> A preponderating element in the type of character to which the evolutionary forces at work in human society are slowly developing, would appear to be the sense of reverence. The qualities with which it is tending to be closely allied are, great mental energy, resolution, enterprise, powers of prolonged and concentrated application, and a sense of simple-minded devotion to conceptions of duty.

138

In the tropics, Kidd implied, white men would develop their mettle.

The strain of thought represented by Pearson and Kidd, which Eric Goldman has labeled "reform Darwinism," became increasingly important as time passed.[24] While conceding to Spencerians that the natural social environment had the character of a jungle, these writers attributed to man the capacity to master it. The pioneer writers stated their case with diffidence, to be sure. Pearson merely described a destiny that would be intolerable unless men strove to make it otherwise, and Kidd went only one step further, outlining a hypothetical method of adaptation to natural forces. Nevertheless they opened for readers a vision of a world with much greater scope for human creativity. Marx had, of course, sketched a similar vision, but in terms appealing mainly to the temperaments of revolutionaries. Pearson and Kidd presented prospects attractive to men who felt themselves thus far the gainers in Spencer's struggle for survival. Oversimplifying and enlarging on their basic idea, which other writers meanwhile developed in more sophisticated terms, the generations coming to command in Western countries attempted by many means to improve on the products of natural law. The expansion into the tropics advocated by Pearson and Kidd became only one prescription among many. Initially, however, it stood as almost the only practical suggestion, aside from Marx's, of a means by which men might attempt to control their futures.

Many ideas found expression in writings of the seven-

[24] Eric Goldman, *A Rendezvous with Destiny* (New York, 1952), pp. 93–97.

ties, eighties, and nineties. Leroy-Beaulieu, Fabri, and Froude contested the view that colonies were valueless. In addition to pointing out economic benefits, the continental writers, supplemented by Mahan, stressed the uses of colonies for the state. Putting the case in quite different terms, Dilke, Seeley, Fiske, and Froude emphasized the benefits conferred on colonial peoples and the rewards piled up in heaven by Europeans who did the conferring.

Pearson and Kidd opened up still another perspective. While accepting all that Dilke and the rest said about spiritual benefits from colonial enterprise, they suggested that these benefits might include amelioration of conditions at home, reduction in class tensions, and postponement or prevention of socialism. Though the view of colonies held by Smith, Bright, Gladstone, Bryce, and Morley remained orthodox among liberals, it no longer held the field alone.

VII

NEW TURNS IN EVENTS

Peorle who write books may too easily assume that books are read. We really know only that the works discussed in the previous chapter had some circulation. Cecil Spring Rice believed Dilke's *Greater Britain* and Curzon's *Problems of the Far East* to be well known in America. Former Secretary of State Bayard received a gift copy of Seeley's *Expansion of England*. Ellis Yarnall read *Oceana*, appropriately, on an ocean voyage. Pearson received from Theodore Roosevelt not only a warm review in print but also a letter saying of *National Life and Character* that no recent work except Mahan's had "excited anything like as much interest or . . . caused so many men to feel that they had to revise their mental estimates of facts." The American edition of Kidd's *Social Evolution* went through ten printings in eleven months.[1] Whether or not such

[1] Stephen Gwynn, ed., *The Letters and Friendships of Sir Cecil Spring*

141

scraps of fact add up to evidence of influence is hard to judge.

Very likely, Americans who kept track of European affairs felt more effect from what they saw than from what they read. If so, during the 1870s they would have found only faint cause for questioning the Bright-Gladstone view of colonies. To be sure, the British North America Act of 1867 improved relations between Britain and Canada and lessened the prospect of their parting company. Also, 100,-000 English workingmen petitioned Queen Victoria to retain the empire, declaring that, whatever the costs and burdens, colonies served as "fields of emigration." [2] As a result some English politicians took issue with prevailing doctrine. They were, however, Englishmen whom most Americans held in low esteem—Disraeli and the Tories.

In a famous speech at the Crystal Palace in 1872 Disraeli assailed the idea of inevitable independence for colonies as "totally passing by those moral and political considerations which made nations, and by the influence of which alone

Rice: A Record, 2 vols. (London, 1929), I, 58, 114; the Earl of Ronald-shay, The Life of Lord Curzon, 3 vols. (London, 1928), I, 203; Charlton Yarnall, ed., Forty Years of Friendship, as Recorded in the Correspondence of John Duke, Lord Coleridge and Ellis Yarnall During the Years 1856 to 1895 (London, 1911), p. 257; Theodore Roosevelt, Works (New York, 1924), XIV (Literary Essays), 230–257; Elting E. Morison et al., eds., The Letters of Theodore Roosevelt, 8 vols. (Cambridge, Mass., 1951–54), I, 376–377. A revised American edition of Social Evolution, with a special preface, appeared in Nov. 1894. A 1902 printing notes on the reverse of the title page that the work had been reprinted in Dec. 1894, Jan., Feb., March, April, May, July, Aug., and Oct. 1895, April 1898, Feb. 1900, and April 1902.

[2] C. A. Bodelson, Studies in Mid-Victorian Imperialism (Copenhagen, 1924), p. 104.

men are distinguished from animals." Conservatives, he said, would seek to nourish and preserve "those distant sympathies which may become the source of incalculable strength and happiness to this land." Although Disraeli actually cared little about colonial possessions, he regarded workers and landowners as natural allies, sharing antagonism toward industrialists, businessmen, and the middle classes, and he evidently thought the theme of the Crystal Palace speech one on which the two groups could unite.[3] After becoming Premier in 1874 he formally proclaimed Victoria Empress of India. By purchasing a controlling interest in the Suez Canal and acquiring Cyprus he added to what by the end of the seventies he called "the Tory empire."

With rare exceptions, even the most conservative Americans regarded English Tories as reactionary, and a pro-Confederacy stand by prominent Tories had recently reinforced this prejudice. As for Disraeli himself, he was a novelist, a wit, a Jew, and the idolized Gladstone's rival for the premiership. For Americans who detested him, as did Charles Eliot, Andrew Carnegie, E. L. Godkin, and Ellis Yarnall, his pro-empire turn probably had the effect of strengthening faith in liberal anticolonialism.[4]

[3] T. E. Kebbel, ed., *Selected Speeches of the Late Right Honourable the Earl of Beaconsfield*, 2 vols. (London, 1882), II, 523–535; W. F. Monypenny and George Earl Buckle, *The Life of Benjamin Disraeli, Earl of Beaconsfield*, 5 vols. (London, 1910–1920), V, 194–196. See Hans Rühl, *Disraelis Imperialismus und die Kolonialpolitik seiner Zeit* (Leipzig, 1935), Bodelson, *Mid-Victorian Imperialism*, pp. 120–124, and Richard Koebner and Helmut Dan Schmitt, *Imperialism: The Story and Significance of a Political Word, 1840–1960* (Cambridge, Eng., 1964), pp. 107–134.

[4] Henry James, *Charles W. Eliot*, 2 vols. (Boston, 1930), I, 179–180;

As the seventies gave way to the eighties, however, the English scene changed. As of 1879–80, Americans had no trouble identifying imperialism with Tories and anti-imperialism with Liberals. Disraeli's ministry had reached the brink of war by upholding, in England's strategic interest, the decaying Ottoman Empire. In faraway Afghanistan it waged war to subdue border tribes. In southern Africa it carried on yet another war to overcome the Zulus. Despite protests from the independent Boer republics thus shut off from the sea, it annexed and added to the Cape Colony the Transvaal.

English Liberals opposed these policies, which Americans labeled both "jingo" and "imperialist." So did Lord Randolph Churchill, the one young Tory in whom, because of his having taken an American bride, Americans took particular interest. Comment in the American press had a delighted "I told you so" tone when in 1880 Churchill broke with Disraeli and, with a handful of other young MPs, formed a fourth party (the third party being that of the Irish nationalists).[5]

Liberals denounced imperialism categorically and unreservedly. In the election campaign of 1880 Gladstone said of Cyprus and the Transvaal that, if they "were as valuable

---

Burton J. Hendrick, *The Life and Letters of Andrew Carnegie*, 2 vols. (Garden City, N. Y., 1932), I, 229; E. L. Godkin, *Reflections and Comments, 1865–1895* (New York, 1895), p. 292; Yarnall, *Forty Years of Friendship*, p. 161.

[5] Winston Spencer Churchill, *Lord Randolph Churchill*, 2 vols. (London, 1906), I, 73; New York *Tribune*, Sept. 8, 1880; Chicago *Tribune*, Sept. 10, 1880; *Nation*, XXXI (Sept. 9, 1880), 182, (Sept. 23, 1880), 216; *Frank Leslie's Illustrated Newspaper*, LI (Sept. 11, 1880), 19.

as they are valueless, I would repudiate them because they are obtained by means dishonourable to this country." He said further of the threatened conflict with the Boers that it placed Englishmen "in the strange predicament of the free subjects of a Monarchy going to coerce the free subjects of a Republic." Bright, William E. Forster, Dilke, Rosebery, and Coleridge, all of whom had American connections, spoke with equal vehemence.[6]

Gladstone won. Forming a Cabinet that included Bright, Forster, and the young Birmingham radical, Joseph Chamberlain, he began to cope with imperial problems. He ordered a pullback in Afghanistan and pursued negotiations for a peaceful settlement with the Boer republics. As these negotiations dragged on without result, however, Gladstone's Cabinet lost its unity. The old Palmerstonian Whigs in it insisted that the Boers be forced to recognize British supremacy; Forster, a onetime abolitionist, held out against retreat from the Transvaal on the ground that surrendering the native Africans to the Boers would be equivalent to handing them over to slavers; only Bright and the young radicals, including Dilke as Undersecretary in the Foreign Office, saw no imperial interest worth defending. The British press commented on the Cabinet's evident division, and so did London correspondents for American newspapers.

The extent of intraparty friction revealed itself early in

[6] John Morley, *The Life of William Ewart Gladstone*, 3 vols. (London, 1904), III, 27–28; Paul Knaplund, *Gladstone and Britain's Imperial Policy* (New York, 1927), pp. 149–153; Ronald Robinson, John Gallagher, and Alice Denny, *Africa and the Victorians* (London, 1961), p. 65.

1881 when the radical ministers abstained from voting with the government on a resolution in favor of coercion in the Transvaal. In this vote Randolph Churchill, the fourth party, and the Irish formed a bloc with the radicals.

This stubborn anti-imperialism seemed to have its effect. American correspondents assumed, it should be remarked, that Gladstone's sympathies lay with the radicals. The Cabinet bent to the will of the dissenters. Despite a battle at Majuba Hill in February 1881, in which Boer irregulars humiliated British forces, the Gladstone government negotiated a pact restoring the Transvaal republic to independence. Though some unsuspected complexities had glimmered, Liberal anti-imperialism still shone with a pure light.[7]

Then the Gladstone Cabinet became involved with the Egyptian problem. The foreign-backed regime in Egypt had become more and more rickety. As the authority of the Khedive waned, that of nationalistic army officers increased. In 1881 came a military revolt, led by Arabi Pasha, which the Khedive could not overcome. The British and French, as joint guardians of Egypt and the Suez Canal, discussed what should be done. Meanwhile Arabi's forces became, at least in appearance, a greater menace to the canal, and in May 1882 rioting at Alexandria resulted in the death of fifty Europeans.

Gladstone's government acted. With the French temporizing, it acted alone. In July 1882 a fleet commanded by

[7] Robinson, Gallagher, and Denny, *Africa and the Victorians*, pp. 68–75; New York *Tribune*, Dec. 14, 1880; *Nation*, XXX (June 3, 1880), 411.

Admiral Beauchamp Seymour bombarded the coastal fortifications at Alexandria, reducing them to powder and killing as many as 2,000 Egyptians.

The news of this action reverberated through the United States. Details about Seymour's eight "monster ironclads," capable with their sixty-six guns of firing a combined broadside of over fifteen tons, filled most American dailies and some weeklies. For years thereafter editors and congressmen would cite the fate of Alexandria when appealing for expenditures on coast defenses or the navy. At the time American comment reflected chiefly wonderment that a Liberal government led by Gladstone could behave in such fashion. While Bright's resignation from the Cabinet suggested that Palmerstonian Whigs had prevailed over genuine Liberals, the continuance in office of Forster, Harcourt, Chamberlain, and Dilke indicated that the explanation might not be quite so simple.

Egyptian affairs then went from bad to worse. The apparent chaos following the bombardment of Alexandria jeopardized the canal and all Europeans still resident in Egypt. Obtaining a special credit of over $10,000,000, the Liberal Cabinet sent an army into Egypt.

Though Gladstone said again and again that his government had no wish to take over Egypt, his efforts to restore stability brought native potentates more and more under English control. British forces thrust deep into the interior to war against still another nationality, the Sudanese led by El Mahdi. A defeat at Omdurman, a thousand miles south of Cairo, led to dispatch of a relief expedition under the romantic mystic, General Charles Gordon, and to the annihilation of Gordon and his men at Khartoum. In American metropolitan dailies, including the Chicago *Tribune* and the St. Louis *Republic*, the disaster at Khartoum drew more news space than had that of General George Custer at the Little Big Horn nine years earlier.

Gladstone still spoke of desiring to get out of Egypt. Even after Khartoum he announced that the Sudan would be evacuated. But by June 1885, when his government fell, he had conceded that withdrawal from Egypt proper would probably not take place for many years.

Nor was Egypt the only new holding that the Liberal government willed its successor. Negotiations defining rights and boundaries in western Africa left Britain with larger domains than before. Though respecting the independence of the Transvaal, the government annexed Bechuanaland in order to keep it from the Boers or European powers that might ally with the Boers. In the Pacific the Liberals took possession of the Fiji Islands.

Steadily, moreover, Gladstone's orations began to sound more and more like passages from Dilke's *Greater Britain*. As early as 1882, he said;

> Let the government adopt, with mathematical rigour if you like, an opposition to annexation, and what does it effect? It does nothing to check that tendency—that, perhaps, irresistible tendency—of British enterprise to carry our commerce and the range and area of our Settlements beyond the

limits of our Sovereignty in these countries where civilisation does not exist.[8]

A similar, even more marked shift occurred among younger English statesmen.

In the early stages of the Egyptian imbroglio Randolph Churchill criticized Gladstone in much the same terms in which he had criticized Disraeli. In 1883, however, he helped to organize the Primrose League. Modeled on masonic orders and fraternal lodges, this league was supposed to bring together aristocrats and workingmen, whom Churchill, like Disraeli, believed to be natural allies. Its charter excluded from membership only "atheists and enemies of the British Empire," and its express objectives embraced "the *Maintenance of Religion* . . . and of the *Imperial Ascendancy of the British Empire!*" Lady Randolph Churchill (the former Jennie Jerome) was Dame President of the League.[9]

In 1885 Churchill ranged himself with radical ex-abolitionists in denouncing Gladstone's decision to withdraw from the Sudan. The government, he said, failed in its duty to the Sudanese and to civilization. Taking the India Office in the Conservative government formed after Glad-

[8] Knaplund, *Gladstone's Imperial Policy*, p. 147. This speech was quoted in the New York *Herald*, March 18, 1882. Since many newspapers used the *Herald's* wire services, it was probably quoted elsewhere, but in a random sampling of other dailies I failed to find it.

[9] Churchill, *Lord Randolph Churchill*, I, 256–258; Mrs. George Cornwallis-West, *The Reminiscences of Lady Randolph Churchill* (New York, 1908), pp. 135–136; Janet H. Robb, *The Primrose League, 1883–1906* (New York, 1942), pp. 106–117.

stone's fall, Churchill directed a campaign to conquer Burma and, in 1886, theatrically announced its annexation as "a New Year's present for the Queen." Not a man to make a fetish of consistency, Churchill sometimes reverted to lines of argument he had used before 1883. Nevertheless he seemed a full convert to imperialism.[10]

Since Churchill had started as a Tory, Americans following his career could discount his conversion by recalling that fact. They could not so easily explain the turn taken in the same direction by Liberals such as Rosebery and Chamberlain.

Having sided completely with Bright in earlier years, Rosebery began to veer away even before the Liberals took power in 1880. During the campaign he spoke of "the great Empire throughout the world, which we are as proud of as any Tory." Working to tighten bonds with the colonies, he helped to form the Imperial Federation League.

With Egypt the center of debate, Rosebery's views went through a further change. Though Undersecretary for Home Affairs, he took an intense interest in Egypt and criticized the Cabinet's vacillation. In 1883 he resigned. A visit to the United States in the autumn gave him opportunity to tell his many New York friends why, in his judgment, Bright's formulas no longer applied.

After serving as Foreign Secretary in the short-lived

[10] Churchill, *Lord Randolph Churchill*, II, 183, gives a good example of Churchill's lack of consistency. Soon after he had become Chancellor of the Exchequer he had to take a position in international monetary negotiations. He turned to an aide, saying, "I forget. Was I a bimetallist when I was at the India Office?"

Gladstone ministry that sponsored home rule for Ireland, Rosebery had special responsibility for questioning Conservative foreign policy. In the House of Lords he goaded the Conservatives for allowing other nations to acquire lands in Africa and islands in the Pacific. He reproached the party in power for not being imperialistic enough.[11]

Chamberlain executed an even more striking reversal. Just as Churchill could be discounted as a Tory, so Rosebery could be held a Whig; but Chamberlain was a radical. Like Bright, he represented Birmingham and, indeed, had had Bright as a political patron. After a successful career in business he had become mayor of the city. His fame reached the United States even at that stage, for he made his administration a model of efficiency and waged a much-publicized battle for nonsectarian education. After entering Parliament he quickly became one of the more forceful critics of Disraeli, and in Gladstone's Cabinet stood second only to Bright in opposing the decisions to bombard Alexandria, post troops to Egypt, and send an expedition into the Sudan.

After the fall of the Gladstone ministry in 1885 Chamberlain's speeches as a private member confirmed rumors that he had dissented on these and other issues. A volume by him, *The Radical Platform*, recommended lines of action much bolder than those endorsed by Gladstone. Though most had to do with domestic affairs, those relating to for-

[11] The Marquess of Crewe, *Lord Rosebery*, 2 vols. (London, 1931), I, 175–176, 195–218, 308–316; New York *Tribune*, Feb. 18, March 3, Dec. 18, 1888.

eign policy took high moral ground.

Chamberlain became the *beau idéal* of cosmopolitan Americans, especially of the younger generation. Godkin lauded him in the *Nation*. Theodore Roosevelt met him and afterward wrote several friends to tell them of the event and of the Englishman's "keen, shrewd intellect and quiet force." Wayne MacVeagh wrote, "I have been in the habit for many years of reading all of Mr. Chamberlain's important speeches. It has been a very remarkable career from the intellectual point of view and I have followed it from Birmingham to his present great position." [12]

Americans applauded nearly all of Chamberlain's stands, and most of all his stand on Ireland, for he ranked ahead of even Morley as a champion of Irish self-government.

Then all at once Chamberlain's position came to seem altogether different. He had advocated greater independence for Irish counties and cities and less coercion by the English government, but not a separate parliament in Dublin. In 1885–86, when the Liberals briefly returned to office and Gladstone startled the world by announcing that the Liberal party now favored such a parliament, with virtual independence for Ireland, Chamberlain refused to support his leader. He not only resigned from the government but left the Liberal party, thereafter commanding a faction that called itself Unionist, insisting on maintenance of the union with Ireland and forming an alliance with the Conservatives. Though Chamberlain remained the sponsor of

[12] *Nation*, XXXVII (July 19, 1883), 48; Morison, *Letters of Theodore Roosevelt*, I, 124–125; MacVeagh to Endicott, Aug. 21, 1893, Private Papers of William C. Endicott, Massachusetts Historical Society.

the Radical Platform, he became identified with what Americans regarded as a reactionary stand on Ireland.[13]

At almost the same time Chamberlain turned imperialist, and did so in circumstances ensuring maximum publicity in the United States. In 1887–88 he came to Washington as a special envoy to settle disputes about American and Canadian fishing rights. Though attacked by Irish-American spokesmen, he won a generally favorable press and made many friends among businessmen and politicians. With the negotiations still in progress and Chamberlain hence still front-page copy in America, he made his first profession of imperialist faith. In a speech in May 1888, he declared:

> We should maintain firmly and resolutely our hold over the territories that we have already acquired, and we should offer freely our protectorate to those friendly chiefs and peoples who are stretching out their hands towards us. . . .
>
> No doubt the burthen of this great Empire is tremendous. . . . But if we face our obligations, if we perform our duties well and faithfully, the honour and the credit will be proportionate to the sacrifices that we may make, while the abandonment of these duties would be as fatal to our material prosperity as it would be discreditable to our national character and our national honour.[14]

[13] On Chamberlain's changes in position, see Garvin, *Chamberlain*, II, *passim*. Examples of American reaction are in *Harper's Weekly*, XXX (June 12, 1886), 371; *Frank Leslie's Illustrated Newspaper*, LXII (June 12, 1886), 259; and the *Nation*, XLII (May 20, 1886), 415.

[14] Garvin, *Chamberlain*, I, 345; Florence E. Gibson, *The Attitudes of*

As a result of marrying Mary Endicott in Washington in November 1888, Chamberlain became for a new reason one of the English statesmen whom Americans watched with special interest. His subsequent speeches received full coverage in American papers, as, for example, when he spoke at Toronto of "the young and vigorous nations carrying everywhere a knowledge of the English tongue and English love of liberty and law" and added that he included the United States among these nations.[15] Later, in speech after speech, he emphasized the benefits of empire and the moral obligation of English-speaking peoples to spread their higher civilization across the globe, and time and again he spoke of the United States as sharing this obligation.

To be sure, Chamberlain's statements about empire had much in common with the statements about Ireland that Americans generally deplored. Strict orthodox liberalism conceded the rightness and wisdom of Ireland's enjoying self-determination. Chamberlain's arguments for union and for colonial empire resembled one another, for he contended that people of common language and a common history should preserve unity at all cost. Some Americans, no matter how much they may have admired Chamberlain's earlier accomplishments, must have reacted against his imperialism because they saw it as of a piece with opposition

the New York Irish Toward State and National Affairs (New York, 1951), pp. 401–422.

[15] Garvin, *Chamberlain*, II, 465; excerpts appeared in the New York *Tribune*, May 15, 1888, New York *Herald*, May 15, 1888, and Chicago *Tribune*, May 16, 1888.

to Irish freedom. Certainly some Irish-Americans did so. To a few, however, Chamberlain's views on colonies may have made appeal precisely because he pictured England and Ireland as counterparts of the American North and South and invoked in support of both his Irish stand and imperialism the example of America's struggle to maintain the Union.[16]

In any case the fact that eminent, responsible political leaders such as Churchill, Rosebery, and Chamberlain accepted and voiced imperialist arguments gave these arguments force with American hearers. Those who viewed London as the great capital could well have concluded that the forward-looking position had its intellectual base not in Mill and the Manchester school but in Dilke, Seeley, or Froude.

Such a tendency would have been reinforced by observation of other capitals, especially Brussels, Paris, and Berlin.

In the late 1870s King Leopold II of Belgium sponsored an International African Association. For a time—until the association became more obviously an instrument for winning King Leopold a personal empire—it seemed to embody and express the *mission civilisatrice* in purest form, aiming at exploration of Africa, suppression of the last vestiges of the slave trade, and the opening of the continent to missionaries and settlers. Addressing the conference that gave birth to the association, Leopold said, "Bringing civilisation to the only part of the earth which it has not yet reached and lightening the darkness in which whole peoples

[16] Garvin, *Chamberlain*, II, 330, 333–334, 402; New York *Herald*, Dec. 31, 1888; Chicago *Tribune*, Dec. 31, 1888.

are plunged is . . . a crusade worthy of this century of progress." [17]

With its linkage to abolitionism, the association inevitably attracted some notice in America. It drew still more attention when Americans became involved in its work.[18] To explore Central Africa, Leopold employed Henry M. Stanley. As an agent for Bennett's New York *Herald*, Stanley had made his celebrated search for the missionary David Livingstone. His reports and his subsequent book, *Through the Dark Continent*, had been read by tens of thousands of Americans. His work for the International African Association added to the association's news value in the United States. So did the presence on its executive committee of another American, Henry S. Sanford, a Connecticut manufacturer and a speculator in Florida real estate, who had been Lincoln's minister to Belgium. Sanford, moreover, made it his business to lobby for the association in Washington and to seek funds for it in other American cities.

As a result Americans heard a good deal about the associ-

[17] Henri Brunschwig, *French Colonialism, 1871–1914: Myths and Realities* (London, 1966), p. 35.

[18] Frank Hird, *H. M. Stanley, The Authoritative Life* (London, 1935), pp. 75–122; Byron Farwell, *The Man Who Presumed: A Biography of Henry M. Stanley* (New York, 1957), pp. 86–94; Ian Anstruther, *Dr. Livingstone, I Presume?* (New York, 1957), pp. 168–181; Robert S. Thomson, "Léopold II et Henry S. Sanford," in *Le Congo: Revue générale de la Colonie Belge*, XI (Oct. 1930), 295–331, and "Léopold II et le Congo, révélés par les notes privées de Henry S. Sanford," *ibid.*, XII (Feb. 1931), 167–196; Edward Younger, *John A. Kasson: Politics and Diplomacy from Lincoln to McKinley* (Iowa City, 1955), pp. 326–336; David M. Pletcher, *The Awkward Years: American Foreign Relations Under Garfield and Arthur* (Columbia, Mo., 1962), pp. 308–324.

ation. They saw what appeared to be jealous rivalry between it and powerful European governments. France, for
example, sent agents to head off Stanley and raise the
French flag over outposts on the Congo River. Then, after
an international conference on Africa in Berlin in 1884–85,
it became increasingly apparent that the association merely
served as a mask for Leopold, with the Congo a colony be-
longing to an individual rather than to a nation.

We do not know whether many Americans drew a moral
from the history of the African International Association.
Certainly it stimulated some to think about roles the United
States might play in Africa. David M. Pletcher, in a study
of the Garfield-Arthur years, quotes one newspaper as suggesting that the Congo might be America's India and another as saying:

> It would be somewhat strange if, in view of all this
> world-wide competition for the new markets of
> Africa, in view of the over-production that is so
> much deplored . . . and in view of the seven mil-
> lions of American Negroes, whose future is such
> an unsettled problem, there should not be many
> more Stanleys, white and black, to seize the oppor-
> tunities which this wonderful continent offers
> with such tempting promises.[19]

John A. Kasson, a former congressman from Iowa, minister to Austria-Hungary for Hayes and to Germany for
Arthur, and a good friend of Sanford, published an article

[19] Pletcher, *The Awkward Years*, p. 322.

in the *North American Review* saying that Americans neglected both economic interest and moral duty by failing to take part in the great work proceeding in Africa.[20] None of this preaching had any direct affect. By declining to ratify the Berlin agreements, Congress renounced a role in African affairs. In the end, publicity about the International African Association had no result except to call attention to Europe's turn toward imperialism.

The new expansionism manifested by France probably surprised Americans even more than did that of Britain. Throughout the 1870s liberal anticolonialism had seemed at its strongest among French republicans, with Leroy-Beaulieu and the geographers who echoed his views standing out as virtual heretics. In 1879, when the young Bonapartist Pretender died fighting with British troops in the Zulu war, the *Nation* published an editorial describing French imperialism, in all senses of the term, as a thing of the past.[21] Yet less than two years later the same magazine had to report not only that imperialism, in the sense of colonial expansion, survived in France but that it had advocates among the staunchest republicans.

In 1880–81 France's Premier was Jules Ferry. One of the three or four French republicans best known in America (Léon Gambetta, Jules Grévy, and Georges Clemenceau being his chief rivals), his fame rested on crusades for free public education waged against the Roman Catholic Church and especially the Jesuit order. Since many Ameri-

---

[20] John A. Kasson, "The Congo Conference and the President's Message," *North American Review*, CXLII (Feb. 1886), 119–133.

[21] *Nation*, XXXI (July 5, 1880), 16.

can Protestants believed themselves faced with similar contests, Ferry enjoyed a good press in America.[22] As Premier, however, Ferry showed himself a colonialist, establishing a protectorate over Tunisia.

Though Ferry's defeat in the Chamber of Deputies in November 1881 appeared to show the French republic's trueness to liberal anticolonialism, his successor, Gambetta, republican of republicans, not only retained control of Tunisia but defended his action as right and wise.

In 1883, with Gambetta dead, Ferry returned to the premiership. Acting as an ambitious and most unapologetic imperialist, he expanded French holdings on the west coast of Africa, raised the French flag over huge tracts in the interior, attempted the conquest of Madagascar, and dispatched an expedition to conquer Tonkin (present-day North Vietnam) and add it to French Indochina.

Military reverses in Madagascar produced mounting criticism of Ferry. A serious defeat in Tonkin brought about his fall. While some of the criticism reflected anticolonial doctrines that had been orthodox a decade earlier, much had a different character. Orators in the Chamber assailed the Premier less for bad policies than for bad timing, saying that he should have waited until revenge had been won against Germany. Though liberal anti-imperialism could still be heard, it had less resonance than in the previous decade.[23]

[22] See, for example, the *Nation*, XXX (Feb. 19, 1880), 129, (March 11, 1880), 187, and *Harper's Weekly*, XXIV (Oct. 16, 1880), 659.

[23] See Brunschwig, *French Colonialism*, pp. 97–104, Thomas F. Power, Jr., *Jules Ferry and the Renaissance of French Imperialism* (New York, 1944), and Martin Aldao, *Les idées coloniales de Jules Ferry* (Paris, 1933).

And Ferry stood forth as an eminent and liberal French republican converted to imperialism. In a famous speech delivered after his fall, he declared:

> For wealthy countries, colonies are places where capital can be invested on the most favorable terms. . . . It must be openly said that the superior races have rights over the inferior races. . . . They have a duty to civilize the inferior races. . . . I assert . . . that our navy and merchant shipping . . . must have safe harbors, defense positions and supply points. . . . A policy of colonial expansion is being engaged in by all the European powers. We must do likewise. If we do not, then we shall meet the fate—not that we here shall experience it, but our children and grandchildren will—which has overtaken other nations which played a great role on the world's stage three centuries ago but which today, for all their greatness and power in the past, are now third- or fourth-rate powers.

Though emphasizing the anticolonial opposition to Ferry, the American press quoted this speech. The press also quoted later speeches and writings by him. Since Levi P. Morton, as American Minister in Paris, had been a friend and admirer of Ferry and had introduced visiting Americans to him, Ferry's example may have had on some Americans an impact comparable to that made on others by Randolph Churchill, Rosebery, and Chamberlain.[24]

[24] Brunschwig, *French Colonialism*, p. 80; New York *Tribune*, July 29, 1885; New York *Herald*, July 30, 1885; McElroy, *Morton*, pp. 131–164.

Germany offered an even more noteworthy instance, for Bismarck, after openly scorning colonies, suddenly set out in the mid-1880s to build an empire.[25] In April 1884 he announced Germany's claim to a large area in southwestern Africa where Britain asserted interest but exercised no effective control. A few months later he stated a similar claim to a portion of New Guinea. In 1885 he added claims to large tracts on the eastern coast of Africa. Through the Berlin conference of 1884–85 and compacts with Britain and Spain, Germany became possessor of empires in Africa and the Pacific.

This sudden turn in policy precipitated debate among German politicians. Certain leaders in the National Liberal party, among them Johannes Miquel and Gustav von Bennigsen, had advocated earlier that Germany acquire colonies. They had done so at a time when their party, once Bismarck's chief reliance in the Reichstag, no longer held the Chancellor's favor. Miquel, Bennigsen, and others therefore hailed the new policy with special fervor because it seemed an omen that Bismarck wanted to revive the old alliance. By the same token, the new policy troubled leaders of the Catholic Center party. Once the targets of a *Kulturkampf* waged by Bismarck with backing from Conserva-

[25] In the large literature on this subject the key works are Mary E. Townsend, *The Origins of Modern German Colonialism, 1871–1885* (New York, 1921); William O. Aydelotte, *Bismarck and British Colonial Policy: The Problem of Southwest Africa, 1883–1885* (Philadelphia, 1937); A. J. P. Taylor, *Germany's First Bid for Colonies, 1884–1885* (New York, 1938); Wolfgang Windelband, *Bismarck und die europäischen Grossmächte, 1879–1885* (Essen, 1940); Erich Eyck, *Bismarck, Leben und Werk*, 3 vols. (Zurich, 1944), III, 394–425; Henri Brunschwig, *L'expansion allemande d'outre-mer* (Paris, 1957); and Walker, *Germany and the Emigration*, pp. 199–239.

tives and National Liberals, they had recently achieved a modus vivendi with the government, and they feared its breakdown if, following their private inclinations, they attacked Bismarck's colonialism. As a result, the new policy had solid but silent support from Conservatives, loud backing from National Liberals, and, in the end, half-hearted endorsement from Ludwig Windthorst, the leader of the Center.

Opposition came from the two parties that had no hope of sharing in a government coalition—Left Liberals led by Ludwig Bamberger, Eugen Richter, and Heinrich Rickert, and Social Democrats. Taking much the line of John Bright, Bamberger, Richter, and Rickert had already attacked Bismarck's protective tariffs and social welfare legislation as state encroachment on zones that ought to be left to individuals. They charged that colonialism had the same character: it jeopardized freedom of emigration, trade, and missionary activity; also, it meant a larger army and navy, subsidies for shippers and traders, and a colonial bureaucracy, all of which entailed more taxes and more surrender of power to the government. The Social Democrats, as Marxists, assailed colonialism as a last desperate attempt by bourgeois capitalism to rescue itself from the inevitable proletarian revolution.

In the Reichstag elections of 1884 Bismarck's colonial policy seemed the chief issue. The parties supporting it won, with the Conservatives gaining a number of Reichstag seats and the National Liberals achieving a large increase in popular vote. Centrists held their own. Left Liberals by

162

contrast lost a third of their seats. Although the Social Democrats made gains, the election's outcome appeared to say audibly that German public opinion favored colonial expansion.[26]

In the United States the parliamentary and electoral debate was covered in greatest detail by the German-language press. Probably cable reports in English-language dailies found readers primarily among Americans of German background, who not only recognized the names of German parliamentary leaders but associated them with events of the past. And to German-Americans the Left Liberals had greatest appeal, for their ranks included prominent forty-eighters, and their cause had editorial support from *Die Nation*, the weekly most respectfully regarded by German-Americans. Relatively speaking, Left Liberal opposition to colonialism received more publicity in the United States than in Germany, and editorials in American newspapers, including those of German Catholics, criticized the National Liberal and Center parties as opportunistic.[27] For most of the German-American community, observation of Germany's debates reinforced faith in the kind of anti-imperialism that Schurz had espoused earlier.

On the other hand, Americans not attuned to German

---

[26] Hans Spellmeyer, *Bismarcks parlamentarische Kämpfe an seine Kolonialpolitik* (Stuttgart, 1931), pp. 14–21; Wilhelm Mommsen, *Johannes von Miquel*, 2 vols. (Stuttgart, 1928), II, 96–98, 141–149, 172–176; Otto Hartwig, *Ludwig Bamberger, eine biographische Skizze* (Marlwig, 1900), pp. 59–60; Theodor Barth, *Politische Porträts* (Berlin, 1904), p. 22; Hans Pehl, *Die deutsche Kolonialpolitik und das Zentrum* (Limburg, 1934).

[27] St. Louis *Herold des Glaubens*, quoted in *New Yorker Staatszeitung*, Oct. 10, 1884.

domestic politics probably found most striking the fact that Bismarck had become an imperialist. In America, as elsewhere, his name was a byword for skillful, realistic, and successful statecraft, and his conversion to imperialism must have caused some Americans to review in their minds the question of whether such a policy was as profitless as anticolonialist doctrine supposed. The outcome of the Reichstag elections suggested further that, at least in Germany, it could also be a popular policy.

Cumulatively, the decade of the 1880s saw in England and on the continent a major shift. Statesmen of the stamp of Churchill, Rosebery, Chamberlain, Ferry, and Bismarck deserted anticolonial doctrines. The governments of Gladstone and Gambetta deserted these doctrines in practice. By observing the behavior of foreign statesmen, Americans who did not read books would have come in touch with such ideas as those of Dilke, Seeley, and Froude. They would also have come in touch with ideas resembling those of Pearson and Kidd, for Chamberlain and Bismarck stood as sponsors not only of imperialism but of ambitious social welfare programs designed to forestall socialism. New conceptions of colonies should have reached not only Americans who read foreign books but also those who merely traveled or kept up with foreign news.

VIII

COLONIALISM IN AMERICA

I<small>N THE EARLY</small> 1880s, when the British moved into Egypt, William Jennings Bryan was a student at Illinois College in Rockford. He wrote his bride-to-be, "However much we may admire England's power in war or her eminence in peace I can not but feel that her foreign policy is mercenary, tyrannical and iniquitous in the extreme and a disgrace to her boasted civilization." [1]

Not long afterward young Theodore Roosevelt published a hastily written biography of Thomas Hart Benton. In it he commented on prospects for annexing Canada and contrasted European and American styles of expansion. Referring to Canada's western provinces, Roosevelt wrote, "Of course no one would wish to see these, or any other settled communities, now added to our domain by force; we

[1] Paolo E. Coletta, *William Jennings Bryan* (Lincoln, Neb., 1964), I (*Political Evangelist, 1860–1908*), 25.

want no unwilling citizens to enter our Union." He continued, "European nations war for the possession of thickly settled districts which, if conquered, will for centuries remain alien and hostile to the conquerors; we, wiser in our generation, have seized the waste solitudes that lay near us." [2]

That Bryan and Roosevelt, in so many respects opposites, held such similar views on colonies illustrates the extent of consensus. As of the early 1880s educated Americans nearly all doubted the value of colonies and regarded efforts to conquer other populations as morally wrong. By the mid-1880s their unanimity had begun to break down.

Nicholas Longworth Anderson, a figure in Washington high society, wrote his son, "Are not the troubles in the Soudan terrible? Without discussing the political right of England to send an army there, my whole sympathy is with her. What pluck! What deeds of marvelous daring! The tight little island queens it over the whole world, and leads commerce and civilization in the by-paths and across the deserts." Ellis Yarnall wrote regretfully to his friend, Coleridge, "There are good people here now who follow Gladstone rather than Bright." The popularity of Fiske's "Manifest Destiny" lecture, sales of Strong's *Our Country*, and the fact that so cosmopolitan a man as Andrew D. White could admit to being impressed by Strong's book suggested greater open-mindedness about colonial expansion than had been the rule earlier.[3]

[2] Theodore Roosevelt, *Thomas Hart Benton* (Boston, 1886), pp. 266–267.
[3] Isabel Anderson, ed., *The Letters and Journals of General Nicholas Longworth Anderson* (New York, 1942), pp. 240–241; Charlton Yarnall,

By the late eighties Thomas J. Coolidge and Lew Wallace, who had had no doubts earlier, had begun to weigh in their minds arguments for annexation of West Indian islands. Coolidge ended up not changing his view. Wallace, on the other hand, began to say that the United States should consider developing a Western Hemisphere federation.[4]

Yarnall, in his letters to Coleridge, turned like a weather vane. In 1891 he wrote, "What a glory it is for England that she has founded this great empire . . . that she has given law and order and wise government to the near 300 millions of India!" With regard to the British role in Egypt he wrote somewhat later, "Never was work done by a civilized nation, in behalf of an oppressed foreign population, nobler and more effective. . . . I wish my country could point to any such noble work done outside her own borders."[5]

In 1893, when the Hawaiian revolution created a practical issue, Americans did not react quite as they would have a decade earlier.

Boston newspapers reported Endicott as favoring annex-

---

ed., *Forty Years of Friendship, as Recorded in the Correspondence of John Duke, Lord Coleridge and Ellis Yarnall During the Years 1856 to 1895* (London, 1911), p. 269. Walter LaFeber, *The New Empire: An Interpretation of American Expansion, 1860–1898* (Ithaca, 1963), p. 80, reports that the Cornell University Library copy of *Our Country* bears the notation, "An exceedingly valuable and interesting little book. ADW, April 3, 1887."

[4] Thomas Jefferson Coolidge, *Autobiography* (Boston, 1902), pp. 133–136; Irving McKee, *"Ben-Hur" Wallace, The Life of General Lew Wallace* (Berkeley, Calif., 1947), p. 234.

[5] Yarnall, *Forty Years of Friendship*, pp. 314, 340.

ation and Coolidge, then Minister in Paris, as believing that it would enhance America's standing in Europe. Minot Savage preached a sermon and addressed the Middlesex Club, saying that the Hawaiian bid evidenced the Anglo-Saxon's march toward destiny. Brooks Adams spoke to the Boston *Globe* of America's inevitable advance into the Pacific. Lodge, though a freshman senator, quickly became an advocate of annexation, citing the nation's strategic and economic interests, and Hoar, the senior senator, reportedly shared this view.[6]

In New York, Horace Porter addressed the Union League Club, mentioning with approval the probability that the Harrison administration would annex Hawaii. Reid's *Tribune* led the press in publishing proannexation editorials and cited lawyers Evarts, Choate, and Coudert as supporters. Holls advised his German friends that acquisition of Hawaii would not only strengthen the United States but permit its playing a larger role in the maintenance of world peace. In a widely publicized sermon MacArthur celebrated the beginning of Christianity's march toward Asia. On much the same ground Lyman Abbott endorsed annexation in the *Outlook*.[7]

In Chicago fewer voices spoke for annexation. Judge Caton did so emphatically but appeared to be the only local

[6] Boston *Journal*, Jan. 31, Feb. 2 and 5, 1893; Boston *Herald*, Feb. 1, 9, and 12, 1893; Boston *Globe*, Feb. 5, 1893.

[7] New York *Tribune*, Jan. 31, Feb. 6 and 7, 1893; New York *Herald*, Feb. 1, 5, 6, and 7, 1893; New York *Sun*, Feb. 2, 1893; Brooklyn *Eagle*, Feb. 2, 1893; *Outlook*, XLVII (Feb. 18, 1893), 309–310; Alfred Vagts, *Deutschland und die Vereinigten Staaten in der Weltpolitik*, 2 vols. (New York, 1935), II, 618.

figure keenly interested. On the other hand, Chicago papers reported little strong opposition and, at the same time, carried stories telling of proannexation statements by prominent Bostonians and New Yorkers and by Senator Platt of Connecticut, former Secretary of State Bayard, Senator Camden of New Jersey, Don Dickinson, Clark Howell of the Atlanta *Constitution*, and Senator Morgan of Alabama.[8]

Schurz and Von Holst stood almost alone in denouncing the project from the outset. Senator Stanford of California said he did not favor annexation, but did not explain why. On the whole, contrary opinion appeared reserved or skeptical rather than hostile. Godkin asked in the *Nation*, for example, whether the United States would gain from annexation any advantage that it did not already possess.[9]

Eminent cosmopolitan Americans who voiced opinions seemed on the whole to favor annexation of Hawaii. In view of the anticolonial tradition, this reaction surprised writers of editorials. The Indianapolis *Journal*, for example, declared on January 30, 1893, that the United States would, of course, not wish to acquire a colony far out in the Pacific. The next morning, with news columns carrying wire reports on the views circulating in bigger cities, the editorial page contradicted its statement of the day before, asserting that America seemed destined, after all, to take the islands. When making a comparable reversal, the Chicago *Tribune*

[8] Chicago *Tribune*, Jan. 31–Feb. 2, 1893; Chicago *Inter-Ocean*, Jan. 31, Feb. 2 and 5, 1893; Illinois *Staatszeitung*, Jan. 31–Feb. 2, 1893.
[9] *New Yorker Staatszeitung*, Feb. 5, 1893; Chicago *Tribune*, Feb. 1, 1893; *Nation*, LVI (Feb. 6, 1893), 96.

quoted Representative Chipman of Michigan as saying of annexation, "It is the logical outcome and it is favored by too many men of prominence in public life to have another outcome." [10]

Owing to the hesitancy of Grover Cleveland, Chipman's prophecy did not at once come true. Experienced Washington reporters judged that, had the new President not asked for delay, a treaty would have passed the Senate by more than the requisite two-thirds majority.[11] And Cleveland eventually decided against annexation, not because of public opposition but because of indications that native Hawaiians did not want it and evidence that the American minority's revolution had received illicit aid from Harrison's minister in Honolulu and the U.S. Pacific squadron. Cleveland did not oppose colonial expansion per se; he only insisted that the United States be able afterward to show that she had taken territory with clean hands.

To Lodge, Theodore Roosevelt, Holls, Mahan, and others who advocated annexation on political or strategic grounds, the new evidence made no difference. To those who had seen destiny or Providence at work, it did. When Cleveland announced that he would not proceed toward annexation, Lodge and a few others protested. Otherwise the decision provoked little more than a perfunctory partisan outcry.[12]

10 Chicago *Tribune*, Jan. 31, 1893.

11 New York *Herald*, Feb. 6, 1893; Boston *Herald*, Feb. 22, 1893; New York *Tribune*, Feb. 23, 1893; Washington *Post*, Feb. 27, 1893.

12 William A. Russ, Jr., *The Hawaiian Revolution, 1893–1894* (Selinsgrove, Pa., 1959), pp. 281–346, shows how Republicans shifted ground by

At no time can the public interested in the issue have been very large. Except in San Francisco, no metropolitan daily reported extended discussion. Few organizations heard speeches on the subject. (Horace Porter's words before the Union League Club were merely an aside.) Few sermons touched it. Only during the few days after the initial bid and again after the withdrawal of the treaty did newspaper editors, even in San Francisco, see fit to deal with the annexation question as front-page news. No magazine except the new and adventurous *Forum* commissioned and published articles about it.[13]

The relatively small public that took an interest in Hawaii in January and February 1893 seemed to favor acquisition of an island colony. One reason may well have been that many members of it, and certainly leaders of opinion within it, had read Dilke, Leroy-Beaulieu, Seeley, and Froude and observed Gladstone, Gambetta, and Bismarck and liberal imperialist movements in western Europe. In the *Atlantic* Lodge attacked as "colonialism" the respect that American antiexpansionists showed for the thought of Bright, Gladstone, and other British elders. In the same vein, Theodore Roosevelt wrote Mahan: "We have in

---

centering fire not on Cleveland's failure to annex but on his contemplated policy of restoring the deposed native queen to her throne. See also Ernest R. May, *Imperial Democracy: The Emergence of America as a Great Power* (New York, 1961), pp. 20–23.

[13] Alfred Thayer Mahan, "Hawaii and Our Future Sea Power," *Forum*, XV (March 1893), 1–11; James Schouler, "A Review of the Hawaiian Controversy," *ibid.*, XVI (Feb. 1894), 670–679. On the *Forum*, see Frank Luther Mott, *A History of American Magazines*, 4 vols. (Cambridge, Mass., 1939–57), IV, 511–523.

America among our educated men a kind of belated sur-
vivor of the little English movement among the Englishmen
of thirty years back. They are provincials, and like all provincials, keep step with the previous generation of the me-
tropolis." [14] Lodge and Roosevelt marched with Churchill,
Rosebery, Chamberlain, and others of the new generation.

Once again, however, one would oversimplify if he
merely pointed to currents abroad as an autonomous influence on Americans. While reading in foreign works and observation of foreign events affected views on American
problems, consciousness of what was said and done at home
undoubtedly helped to determine what Americans regarded
as relevant and significant. And individual Americans reacted differently both to domestic happenings and to currents and happenings overseas.

The year of Hawaii's near-annexation forms a good point
for a resurvey of various elements in American thought
about colonies. Comparing views expressed about Hawaii
with those expressed twenty-odd years earlier about the
Dominican Republic, one can see clearly how much the entire American perspective had altered.

In the first place, Americans looked back on their own
history from a changed point of view. As of 1870 they had
still seen the United States as an experiment: the only con-
sequential nation without a monarch and a privileged aristocracy, and the only one that attempted to reconcile na-

[14] Henry Cabot Lodge, "Colonialism in the United States," *Atlantic
Monthly*, LI (May 1883), 612-626; Roosevelt to Mahan, Dec. 13, 1897,
in Elting E. Morison *et al.*, eds., *The Letters of Theodore Roosevelt*, 8
vols. (Cambridge, Mass., 1951-54), I, 741.

tional and local interests by means of a federal system. Though suffrage reform in Britain and the revolutions of 1848 on the continent might seem indications that the world would follow America's lead, not all signs pointed to the same outcome, especially in view of the sectional strife that had so recently jeopardized the nation's own future. In these circumstances Americans searched their history for guidelines to survival. Some saw continuous territorial expansion as a key to past and future success and advocated pushing out into the Caribbean. Others felt that past expansion had been organic and that forced growth of a different kind would bring new problems that might well imperil the future.

Two decades later Americans looked out on a different world scene. Britain had continued to evolve toward democracy; France had become a republic; and Germany and Austria-Hungary had in their own ways adopted the federalist principle. Almost everywhere democracy and federalism seemed on the march. Meanwhile the United States had achieved such progress as to seem assured not only of long life but of preeminence among nations. As of 1890 its population exceeded that of any other developed nation except Russia. In production of food crops, beef, pork, and most minerals it already ranked first, and in output of coal, iron, steel, and manufactured goods it promised soon to surpass Britain. With these facts as part of the context, Americans looked differently at their history, seeking to understand what rules of conduct had led not only to domestic success but to leadership in the world.

From this standpoint, past expansion seemed less a means by which America had secured its existence than a means by which it had enlarged the domain of democracy and federalism and obtained the resources requisite for future greatness. This alteration in emphasis did not, of course, change the facts being interpreted. Earlier generations still appeared to have taken only such territory as could be peopled by North American settlers and, in their wisdom, to have acquired no land except on their own continent. But their heirs could look less fearfully than twenty years earlier at the possibility of making a departure from this rule, especially since the case of Hawaii, with a body of American immigrants in control and the forms of a democratic republic, seemed to conform in most respects to continental precedents. If taken by the United States, this republic could be expected to progress from territorial status to statehood. Annexation would thus lead only to extension of the democratic federal system. The fact that this extension would cross three thousand miles of water could be blinked away, partly because it could be seen as a continuation of westward movement. That enthusiasm for annexation could so quickly disappear probably owed something to emergent doubts as to whether, in fact, the Hawaiian republic was democratic and whether, with all its natives and Chinese and Japanese residents, it could successfully be incorporated into the federal union.

Another alteration in perspective had to do, obviously, with the economic needs of the nation. Soaring statistics on farm and factory output gave new keenness to desire for markets. Looking at the past, Americans could reason that their nation's rise to greatness had been due in part to an expanding population of workers and consumers and in part to Europe's hunger for what America could produce. Despite a continual inpouring of immigrants, the Census Bureau's report that the free land frontier had disappeared seemed a signal that numbers of domestic consumers might cease to rise. Meanwhile, imitation of America's protective tariff policy by Germany, Austria-Hungary, and, most recently, France appeared to jeopardize future trade with Europe. Even in the eighties Congress and the press discussed building better economic relations with Latin America and converting the throngs of Asia into buyers of American goods.

In 1893 Hawaii was hardly spoken of at all as a land area that might be exploited by farmers or miners. Only domestic growers of cane and beet sugar, fearing competition, called attention to the territory's natural resources. Most commentary stressed Hawaii's potential role as an entrepôt for trade with the Far East. In his *Tribune* editorial advocating annexation Reid spoke specifically of "necessity for new markets." [15]

Still another change in perspective could be attributed to the spread of Social Darwinism. In urging annexation of the Dominican Republic, Grant had used every conceivable argument, one being that if the United States did not act, another power might do so. Champions of his proposal made little use of this warning, partly because they recognized

[15] LaFeber, *New Empire*, pp. 146–147.

that the United States could defend a Western Hemisphere state without annexing it, but partly too, perhaps, because they had lost the habit of visualizing their nation as a state competing with others for land, population, and power. By 1893, with so much having been said about struggle for survival and about America's outstripping of other powers, Americans may have found it easier to conceive of the United States as a creature contesting with its own kind. Many advocates of Hawaiian annexation contended that if the American government declined the opportunity, Britain or some other power would step in, gaining advantages in territory, strategic position, and trade.[16]

All these changes in outlook grew out of changes in the American scene—twenty years of progress, a transformation in the economy, and incessant writing and sermonizing about "survival of the fittest." When facing the Hawaiian question, even the most Europeanized of American opinion leaders must have reasoned from past American experience and present American needs. Equally, however, those familiar with English and European experience must have seen the American past in a comparative light, measured the interests of the United States to some extent by what other nations believed to be their interests, and interpreted the national duty according to standards of enlightened thought within the Atlantic community.

By 1898, when Hawaiian annexation came up again and the Philippine issue presented itself, much more had been heard and seen across the Atlantic. The works of Pearson

16 See *Public Opinion*, XIV (Feb. 18, 1893), 465 (Feb. 25, 1893), 489.

and Kidd had come out. Colonial societies had made chauvinistic arguments for colonial expansion commonplace.
After initially taking a conservative tack, Germany's new
Kaiser had proclaimed a turn to "world policy," projecting
a Berlin-to-Baghdad railway, renewing activity in southern
Africa, and, most dramatically, seizing a coaling base and
concession at Kiaowchow Bay on the coast of China. With
Gabriel Hanotaux as Foreign Minister, the French republic
embarked on its own "world policy," sending new expedi-
tions into Central Africa and acquiring a sphere of influence
in southern China.

British governments meanwhile enlarged their domains in
east central Africa and tightened their economic vise on the
Boer republics, thus seeming to follow Cape Colony Prime
Minister Cecil Rhodes's prescription that the Union Jack
should fly from the Cape to Cairo. Responding to Germany's seizure of Kiaowchow Bay, a Salisbury-Chamberlain Cabinet also acquired a new holding in China, the port
of Wei-hai-wei. Czarist Russia, though not seeking foot-
holds in Africa, pressed eastward against the frontiers of
China and, following the German lead, took possession of a
base and concession at Port Arthur on the Manchurian
coast. Nor did the scramble for empire involve only major
powers. Italy joined in, reaching out to conquer Ethiopia
and recoiling only when Ethiopian tribesmen defeated her
armies at Adowa in 1896. Japan took from China the island
of Formosa and established claims to special rights in Korea.

As of early 1898 only four great states were not expanding their empires: China, a victim of the others; Turkey,

the traditional "sick man of Europe"; the rickety Austro-Hungarian empire; and the United States.

Until 1898 few Americans drew the moral that their nation was in the wrong company. Indeed, during most of the nineties Americans reacted to European imperialism defensively rather than imitatively, evidencing most of all fear lest European powers carry their expansion into the Western Hemisphere. This fear could take aggressive form, to be sure. Demanding that Britain refrain from seizing territory in dispute between British Guiana and Venezuela, Olney, as Secretary of State, asserted that in the Western Hemisphere "the United States is practically sovereign . . . and its fiat is law." While this and other refurbishings of the Monroe Doctrine had imperialist undertones, neither Olney nor others contemplated enlargement of the area over which the American flag would hang and in this respect differed from their counterparts abroad.

The same held true with regard to what Lord Charles Beresford called "the break-up of China." Though the Kiaowchow, Port Arthur, and Wei-hai-wei seizures certainly excited some alarm about the future of the Chinese market, no Americans spoke for acquiring a comparable port. The nearest approach came in the New York *Journal of Commerce* editorial mentioned earlier, which took events in China as a point of departure and called for revival of the Hawaiian annexation project. As for China itself, the *Journal of Commerce* and other interested papers held that the United States should seek only free access for American products.[17]

[17] Pratt, *Expansionists of 1898*, pp. 261–268; Charles S. Campbell, *Spe-*

178

While the absence of imperialist clamor like that in Europe might seem evidence that discussion and events abroad had little effect on Americans, this fact probably has a simple explanation. Writings and examples of the 1880s had impact because most of the men making a case for colonies accepted the premises and conclusions of liberalism. Even firm anti-imperialists such as Andrew Carnegie and Charles W. Eliot could find it in themselves to admire Chamberlain and praise Britain's accomplishments in Egypt.[18]

The continental imperialists had a different appearance. From the beginning they emphasized the interests of the state. As time went on they laid less and less stress on economic rewards and more on returns in power and glory. Spokesmen for colonial societies often came from the armed forces or the higher civil service, not the middle class. Even when the new Germany had most admirers in the United States, the power of its officer caste drew criticism. So did that of France, especially after the Dreyfus affair. Looking at imperialist movements on the continent, Americans increasingly made associations with things they disliked, such as statism, militarism, and reaction.

Nor did the example of England offset these impressions. Sitting in the Cabinet as Colonial Secretary from 1895 onward, Chamberlain coupled with his expansionist policies

---

cial Business Interests and the Open Door Policy (New Haven, 1951), pp. 1–18; Thomas McCormick, "Insular Imperialism and the Open Door: The China Market and the Spanish-American War," Pacific Historical Review, XXXII (May 1963), 155–169; Marilyn B. Young, "American China Policy, 1895–1901," unpubl. diss. (Harvard, 1963).

[18] Burton J. Hendrick, The Life and Letters of Andrew Carnegie, 2 vols. (Garden City, N. Y., 1932), I, 430; Henry James, Charles W. Eliot, 2 vols. (Boston, 1930), II, 120–121.

little of the reforming zeal he had shown earlier. In Parliament, in the press, and in such bodies as the Primrose League, right-wing Tories and retired naval officers emerged as the ardent champions of colonial extensions in Africa and of such moves as the seizure of Wei-hai-wei. Even Albert Shaw, a convinced believer in colonialism, grew critical. Using the term with some of its earlier connotations, Shaw called the Salisbury-Chamberlain government too "imperialistic." [19]

Witnessing these trends, American opinion leaders could well have felt less drawn than in 1893 to the idea of America's becoming a colonial power. When debate on Hawaii resumed in the late winter of 1897–98 such seemed the case. By that time the question of whether or not to annex had become a party question. Since a Republican administration had negotiated the original annexation treaty and a Democratic administration had not only rejected the treaty but impugned the methods of the Republican negotiators, Republicans had no choice but to defend the project, and though actual enthusiasts remained few, party platforms endorsed annexation.

When a Republican President came into office in 1897, with a heavy majority in the Senate, the handful of enthusiasts could insist that the project be revived. They did so, and the McKinley administration drew up a new annexation treaty. But ratification required votes from Democrats as well as Republicans. After the European moves in China

[19] Herman Ausubel, *In Hard Times: Reformers among the Late Victorians* (New York, 1940), p. 256.

and the opening of the campaign for annexation by the New York *Journal of Commerce* one senator judged only two or three votes to be lacking.[20] Still, these votes did not materialize.

Given the circumstances, this lack of the necessary Senate votes seems evidence that senators sensed some effective opinion against annexation. Most Republicans would have been governed by party commitment and the wishes of the new President. As a senior member of the Foreign Relations Committee, Lodge could mobilize them. The senior Democrat on the Committee, Morgan of Alabama, could endorse annexation in order to further his pet project of an interoceanic canal. Having broken with Cleveland over the currency issue, most other Democrats felt no moral requirement to uphold the former President's position, and should have been willing to trade with Lodge or Morgan on easy terms. In fact, party line alone would explain opposition only by a dozen or so Cleveland Democrats. The other twenty-odd senators who declined to support annexation must have been influenced either by personal conviction or by evidence that opinion leaders in their constituencies would frown on a proannexation vote. The situation in the Senate indicated that anti-imperialist feeling ran more strongly among the interested public than it had in 1893.

In May 1898, when the Philippines suddenly entered the discussion, evidence of such feeling became plainer. Schurz, who had consistently opposed Hawaiian annexation, spoke out vigorously. So did Sigel and Von Holst. All three char-

[20] LaFeber, *New Empire*, p. 366.

acterized retention of the Philippines as unthinkable. German-American newspapers quickly echoed their statements, expressing incredulity that any Americans could take a different view and suggesting that men who did so had corrupt motives or were drunk or insane.[21]

In Boston, Coolidge, Eliot, Elder, Gargan, and Van Ness all assumed positions much like those taken by Schurz and Sumner in 1869–71. Showing some evidence of having listened to debate on imperial federation, Coolidge ascribed America's strength to the union of free, self-governing states. To assume control over any subject territory would weaken the nation, he felt, while admission of Hawaiians or Filipinos as potential equals would corrupt it. Taking a similar stand, President Eliot of Harvard characterized all reasoning to the contrary as "contemptible." Samuel Elder, the lawyer, and Collins and Gargan, the Irish-American leaders, appealed simply to the national tradition. Van Ness, in a sermon to his Unitarian congregation, condemned lust for conquest.[22]

In New York, Depew, Hewitt, Dodge, Coudert, and Low invoked the arguments of John Bright, describing colonies as expensive and burdensome. Bourke Cockran, like Collins and Gargan, appealed to tradition.[23]

[21] *New Yorker Staatszeitung*, May 5, 12, and 28, 1898; Illinois *Staatszeitung*, May 2 and 7, 1898. For a survey of the German newspapers, see *Literary Digest*, XVII (Aug. 6, 1898), 156–158.

[22] Boston *Advertiser*, May 5 and 8, 1898; Boston *Globe*, May 6, 8, 10, and 16, June 5, 1898; Boston *Herald*, May 3, 4, 8, and 10, 1898; Boston *Pilot*, May 7, 9, and 14, 1898; Coolidge, *Autobiography*, pp. 312–313; James, *Eliot*, II, 123–124.

[23] New York *Herald*, New York *Tribune*, *New York Times*, New

In Chicago, Von Holst spoke so vehemently and dogmatically against expansion that others appeared hesitant about too closely identifying themselves with him. Franklin MacVeagh, Melville Stone, H. H. Kohlsaat, Sigmund Zeisler, Presidents Harper and Rogers of the University of Chicago and Northwestern University, and Rabbi Emil Hirsch merely indicated doubt about the wisdom of acquiring colonies. They did not explain their reasoning.[24]

In Indianapolis, lawyer John Lewis Griffiths spoke for the same point of view, citing specifically the wisdom of John Bright. Meanwhile newspapers in the city, like those in other cities, quoted former Secretary of State Sherman as opposing colonies on grounds of expense, danger, and departure from precedent. They also quoted Bayard, taking a different stand from that of 1893, as seconding the position of Sherman.[25]

Those who expressed anticolonial convictions constituted a majority of the observable local and national opinion leadership.

Many, however, spoke only of the Philippines. Just a few expressed opposition to the pending Hawaiian treaty, and a

---

York *World*, and Brooklyn *Eagle*, May 3, 6, and 7, 1898; *New Yorker Staatszeitung*, May 8, 1898; New York *Irish-American*, May 16, 1898; New York *Irish World*, May 16, 1898; New York *World*, May 15, 1898; Brooklyn *Eagle*, May 16, 1898.

[24] Chicago *Inter-Ocean*, May 3, 8, and 11, 1898; Chicago *Times-Herald*, May 2, 3, 5, 7, 8, 11, and 25, 1898; Chicago *Tribune*, May 2, 8, 12, and 19, 1898; Illinois *Staatszeitung*, May 7 and 9, 1898.

[25] Indianapolis *News*, May 9, 1898. Sherman's statement was reported in most dailies on May 17 or May 18, 1898, Bayard's on May 28 or May 29, 1898.

minority meanwhile pressed with renewed earnestness for annexation of Hawaii. On the whole, the reasoning of this minority did not resemble that of European colonialists and English Tories. The nearest approach came in statements by Mahan and Lodge, justifying Hawaiian annexation primarily in terms of naval requirements. But not even Lodge contended, as did many Europeans, that a state owed it to itself to achieve maximum relative power and that a colony was an increment of power. He spoke instead in the language of Dilke, Seeley, Fiske, Froude, Rosebery, and the early Chamberlain, stressing destiny, charity, duty, and moral self-fulfillment. Most statements favoring colonial expansion sounded these strains.

Richard Olney struck the keynotes in an *Atlantic* article, "The International Isolation of the United States." [26] Though written earlier, the article appeared in print just after Dewey's victory and commanded extraordinary attention. Olney said:

> [The United States ought] to recognize the changed conditions and to realize its great place among the powers of the earth. It behooves it to accept the commanding position belonging to it, with all its advantages on the one hand and all its burdens on the other. It is not enough for it to vaunt its greatness and superiority and to call upon the rest of the world to admire and be duly im-

[26] Richard Olney, "International Isolation of the United States," *Atlantic*, LXXXI (May 1898), 577–588.

pressed. The mission of this country . . . is not merely to pose but to act—and, while always governing itself by the rules of prudence and common sense and making its own special interests the first and paramount objects of its care, to forego no fitting opportunity to further the progress of civilization.

Bringing in a practical argument, Olney spoke of "the present crying need of . . . more markets and larger markets for the consumption of the products of the industry and inventive genius of the American people . . . ," adding, "But our material interests only point in the same direction as considerations of a higher and less selfish character."

President Capen of Tufts saw similar logic for annexation of Hawaii and retention of at least a foothold in the Philippines. "Some say this is imperialism . . . ," he added later, "I am not frightened by an epithet." [27]

Senator Platt of Connecticut came closer than either Olney or Capen to an exact recapitulation of the liberal imperialist case as it had been presented in England. Speaking of "Anglo-Saxon destiny," he declared that the onward progress of law and civilization could not be stayed.[28]

In the New York *Tribune* Whitelaw Reid took the same position. One editorial, entitled "The New Imperialism," distinguished between America's expansion and that of

[27] Boston *Advertiser*, May 6, 1898; Boston *Globe*, June 26, 1898.

[28] Boston *Advertiser*, May 5, 1898. See Louis A. Coolidge, *An Old-Fashioned Senator, Orville H. Platt of Connecticut* (New York, 1910), pp. 287–295.

power-hungry European states. A second, entitled "Missionary Nations," dwelt on the good that America could do and the moral profits that would be earned by doing good without thought of material return.[29]

Robert S. MacArthur developed the latter theme not only in a sermon to his Baptist parishioners but also in a much-publicized speech before the American Tract Society. In Chicago, lawyer Lambert Tree spoke of "duty that Providence has imposed on us." In Indianapolis, manufacturer Hugh Henry Hanna told the local Commercial Club that Europeans looked on Americans as "moneygrubbers" but that Americans would prove them wrong by helping to shoulder the burden of spreading civilization of the uncivilized.[30]

On the fringes of the minority speaking for and not against colonial expansion stood a small group sounding the themes of Pearson and Kidd. In New York, R. Heber Newton and Lyman Abbott both preached sermons saying that the United States should expand in order to purify itself internally.[31]

The imperialist chorus thus had several different and inharmonious parts: one stressing potential gain in power and wealth; another making the point that colonies might help to solve some domestic problems; and a main body reciting fatalistically of duty to be performed, material benefits that would go mostly to colonials, and profit for Americans

[29] New York *Tribune*, May 15 and 17, 1898.

[30] *Ibid.*, May 12 and 16, 1898; Chicago *Tribune*, May 28, 1898; Indianapolis *Journal*, May 17, 1898.

[31] New York *Tribune* and New York *Herald*, May 8 and 16, June 6, 1898.

chiefly in awareness of doing God's will.

With a substantial part of the establishment rejecting all elements of this logic, one would think that the arguments for colonies should have faded out of view. Quite the reverse occurred.

Through the month of May, reporters and politicians sought guidance from the same men whom they had consulted in the early days of the Hawaiian debate of 1893—the Bostonians, New Yorkers, Chicagoans, and others whom we surveyed in earlier chapters. Then, in early June, the press began to give comparable attention to statements by other men, a few of whom had spoken out concerning the Venezuela boundary dispute or the Cuban revolution but most of whom possessed no evident qualifications for speaking about colonies. In general they lacked the cosmopolitan backgrounds typical of men whose opinions on colonies had received publicity earlier.

This new group included some successful businessmen. In Boston, for example, the president of the Chamber of Commerce, the head of the Boston Marine Society, a member of the Harbor and Land Commission, and a merchant from Salem all told the *Globe* that they favored expansion into the Pacific for economic reasons. Albert Clarke, a lobbyist for New England manufacturers, endorsed the same policy, but, instead of using Lodge's grounds, borrowed those of Reid and MacArthur, saying, "we have extraterritorial responsibility. It differs from imperialism in the sense that it is not aggrandizement but duty." [32]

More conspicuous than businessmen were clergymen.

[32] Boston *Globe*, June 5, 12, and 26, 1898.

Through June 1898 the numbers of proexpansion sermons seemed to increase Sunday by Sunday.[33] Meanwhile editorials in newspapers took a similar turn. Chauncey Depew declared:

> In my daily business I have clipped out for me reports in the papers from all over the country. Every morning they are placed before me, so that I may see how things that may have some bearing on the railroad business are going. I can't help seeing what a strong feeling is spreading over the whole land in favor of colonial expansion.[34]

Albert Shaw, who, as editor of the *Review of Reviews*, read a large sample of the press, wrote at the end of May that the "predominant opinion of thoughtful men now seems to be that we want to hold the Hawaiian Islands as a permanent possession, but that we want to get out of the Philippines as soon as we can safely and honorably withdraw." A month later Shaw exclaimed over "the remarkable vigor and extent of the American sentiment in favor of the permanent retention of the [Philippine] islands."[35] Soon the weekly press surveys *Public Opinion* and *Literary Digest* could reproduce large numbers of editorials: in August *Public Opinion* reported 28 papers for annexation of the Philippines, 21 others leaning in that direction, and only 16 opposing; in early September the *Literary Digest* named 147 papers that

[33] See Pratt, *Expansionists of 1898*, pp. 291–316; *Religious Review of Reviews*, II (July 1898), 372; *ibid.*, III (Aug. 1898), 431–436, 469–470; *ibid.*, IV (Jan. 1899), 846.

[34] St. Louis *Republic*, May 17, 1898.

[35] *Review of Reviews*, XVIII (June 1898), 654; *ibid.* (July 1898), 16.

favored keeping all or part of the archipelago as against 45 calling for some other course. Meanwhile, as Pratt has described, the same trend appeared in business and religious periodicals.[36]

Politicians began to view effective public opinion as leaning toward expansion. Circumspect at first, many representatives and senators declined to answer questions put to them during May about Hawaii. Some said they would vote for annexation but took pains to add that they felt no commitment to go further. Typifying the cautious attitude of professional politicians, Pennsylvania's Republican senator, Boies Penrose, said early in June:

> Neither in our suddenly acquired position in the affairs of the world nor in our desire for trade extension is there as yet, and I hope there never will be, any sentiment among our people for mere territorial acquisition; but there is a well-defined sentiment . . . that the United States should acquire such territory, like the islands of Hawaii, as is absolutely necessary . . . for the better protection of the American continent from foreign aggression and for the promotion and extension of our foreign commerce.[37]

To avoid a possible defeat in the Senate, supporters of Hawaiian annexation had turned to the device of a joint resolution. Coming to the floor of the House in mid-June, it won

[36] *Public Opinion*, XXV (Aug. 4, 1898), 132–135; *Literary Digest*, XVII (Sept. 10, 1898), 307–308; Pratt, *Expansionists of 1898*, pp. 268–278, 289–316.

[37] Philadelphia *Public Ledger*, June 3, 1898.

by more than two-to-one. Three weeks later the Senate voted for annexation by much the same margin.

Before the Senate vote the chiefs of the Democratic party's warring factions both spoke. Cleveland came out more strongly than ever before against acquiring colonies. Bryan, theretofore silent, adopted an equally firm anticolonial stand.[38] Though both men undoubtedly expressed real convictions, both spoke also as practical politicians, seeking not only to reunite the Democratic party but also to attract support from German-Americans and other outspoken antiexpansionists who, as Mugwumps, had deserted Republican ranks once before. Their statements reflected an evident calculation that the public really interested in and favorable to expansion remained relatively small. In spite of support of Hawaiian annexation by southern and western Democratic congressmen and newspapers, Cleveland and Bryan obviously did not expect to alienate large numbers of loyal Democrats. Presumably, both men judged any such losses likely to be more than made up by gains elsewhere.

The caution with which Republican leaders approached the Philippine issue indicated similar assumptions about the size of the interested public. In drawing up platforms at state conventions, they chose for the most part to avoid commitment. Thirteen such platforms called for keeping some or part of the archipelago, while thirty-two preserved silence.[39] Together with McKinley's slowness in reaching a decision, this evidence suggests that Republican leaders re-

[38] New York *World*, June 22 and 25, 1898.
[39] *Literary Digest*, XVII (Oct. 22, 1898), 481–482.

mained unsure about several factors: the numbers of voters actually eager for colonial expansion; the numbers of these so loyal that they would turn out even if the party opposed expansion; and the numbers of antiexpansionists who cared less about the colonial question than about the gold standard, the tariff, or some other Republican cause.

Lacking any explicit estimates from politicians of the time, we can only guess as to the size of the public interested in the Hawaiian or Philippine questions. Since some speeches, sermons, and editorials treated expansion as a matter of morality or domestic economic or political need, the public should probably not be conceived as exclusively a foreign policy public. On the other hand, the numbers in it cannot have been much greater than the maximum foreign policy public, which was 3–4 million at the outside.

Whatever the figure, this public outnumbered that which had been interested in Hawaii in 1893. It appeared to grow continuously larger during June, July, and August 1898, and as it grew, seemed to be represented by and responsive to a larger and more varied group of opinion leaders.

I X

SOME TENTATIVE
EXPLANATION

Wᴵᴛʜ ᴍᴏsᴛ ʟᴇᴀᴅᴇʀs of opinion initially opposing imperialism, how and why did a swelling public come to support the taking of the Philippines?

In trying to answer this question one has to keep in mind the factors stressed by Merk, Pratt, LaFeber, and Hofstadter. With their thoughts turned to Hawaii or the Philippines, many Americans may have called up memories of Manifest Destiny. Mentioning Jefferson, Jackson, and Polk, a San Francisco daily declared that the "virile yeomanry of the Democratic party" would not follow "bloodless pedagogues of the Mugwump stripe." Murat Halstead of the Cincinnati *Commercial* said, "The world has just grown ripe for policies of annexation by all the great powers, and we are one of them. . . . 'We the people of the United

States' never lost liberty or any good thing from acquiring good land, and never will." [1]

As Pratt discovered, many business and religious periodicals employed Social Darwinist language. Many editorials in church organs described America's alternatives as expansion or decline. Mingling Calvinism and Darwinism, many also portrayed expansion as predestined. Even the *Catholic World*, with many Irish and German-American subscribers, spoke of the dynamism of the Anglo-Saxon race leading inevitably to territorial expansion.[2]

Many periodicals also cited new conditions created by technological developments. Calling for annexation of the Philippines, the *Baptist Union* remarked, "The century that is just closing has brought with it great changes. There are no longer any far-off lands. . . . Steam and electricity have well-nigh blotted out distance." [3]

As both Pratt and LaFeber point out, the business press constantly emphasized the nation's need for new commercial opportunities. Echoing this theme, business organizations urged the government to help open foreign markets. The New York State Bankers' Association, for example, resolved:

> Our capacity to produce far exceeds our capacity
> to consume. The home market can no longer keep
> furnaces in blast or looms in action. That capital

[1] *Literary Digest*, XVII (Aug. 27, 1898), 340; *Public Opinion*, XXIV (June 30, 1898), 807.
[2] *Catholic World*, LXVII (June 1898), 426.
[3] *Baptist Union*, VIII (May 14, 1898), 338.

may earn its increment and labor be employed, enterprise must contend in the markets of the world, for the sale of our surplus products.[4]

In coming to an opinion about colonial expansion many Americans unquestionably thought of the depressed economic conditions of recent years, the shrinkage of foreign markets resulting from European tariffs, and the prospect of expanded trade if the United States had island colonies as entrepôts in the Far East.

Underlying some of the public response may have been other, less rational impulses. Several years of severe depression had brought declines in sales, fees, commissions, and salaries, causing many in the middle class to falter in their lockstep with the Joneses. Those actually falling back felt themselves encroached upon by advancing immigrant minorities, deemed to be socially inferior. As Hofstadter and others have argued, the resultant heightened anxiety could have had an influence not only on the movement for war with Spain but on later responsiveness to imperialism. Contemporary psychologists, it is true, have not had much luck in proving connections between status insecurity and aggressive stands on foreign policy issues. The best study shows equal correlations with elements of childhood history, attitudes toward parents, and certain kinds of perceptions and values.[5] Larger-scale surveys, such as the famous inquiry into "the authoritarian personality," have used

4 *Rand-McNally Banker's Monthly*, XVI (Aug. 1898), 143.
5 M. Brewster Smith, Jerome S. Bruner, and Robert H. White, *Opinions and Personality* (New York, 1956).

questionable methods.[6] Still, it remains conceivable that worry over social status translated itself somehow into approval of colonialism, and hence that the "psychic crisis" entered into play along with the Manifest Destiny tradition. Social Darwinism, technological change, and yearning for new markets.

To tick off factors encouraging expansionism is still, however, to touch only a segment of the problem. Assuming that interested citizens arrived at opinions partly through influence from others, one still has to explain how opinion in favor of expansion took root when the largest part of the establishment advised otherwise. Why were expansionist impulses not smothered as in 1869–71?

The two situations, of course, differed. In the earlier period opponents of annexation had been able to recommend doing nothing. In 1898 they had to advocate returning the Filipinos to Spanish rule, handing them over to another power, or launching them on a chancy experiment with independence. While the earlier debate came in the aftermath of a long and wearing war, that of 1898 occurred with a

[6] T. W. Adorno, Else Frankel Brunswick, D. J. Levinson, and R. N. Sanford, *The Authoritarian Personality* (New York, 1950). The most devastating critiques are in Richard Christie and Marie Jahoda, eds., *Studies in the Scope and Method of "The Authoritarian Personality"* (Glencoe, Ill., 1954), and Gerhard E. Lenski and John C. Leggett, "Caste, Class and Deference in the Research Interview," *American Journal of Sociology*, LXV (March 1960), 463–467. Nevertheless the F. Scale developed by Adorno and his colleagues has been used with some effect in subsequent surveys. See the bibliographical note on pp. 103–104 of Ernest R. May, "An American Tradition in Foreign Policy: The Role of Public Opinion," in William H. Nelson and Francis L. Loewenheim, *Theory and Practice in American Politics* (Chicago, 1964), pp. 101–122.

195

war just begun and patriotic nationalism on the bubble. And, as Pratt and LaFeber would emphasize, many changes had meanwhile occurred in the thinking of Americans and structure of the American economy.

But not to be forgotten are changes that had come over the world scene. In 1898 the fashionableness of imperialism abroad cropped up again and again in American commentary. When Kohlsaat's Chicago *Times-Herald* came out for expansion, its editorial pointed to the English example and the proexpansionist advice of such men as Henry Norman. The *Baptist Home Mission Monthly*, speaking of Spain's expulsion from the Philippines as a *sine qua non*, asserted, "Nothing short of this will satisfy the enlightened public sentiment of this country—and of England." Albert J. Beveridge called for advancing into the world "as our mother has told us how." Hamlin Garland, the novelist, confessed to questioning the anti-imperialism current among his agrarian friends largely because of a conversation with Rudyard Kipling.[7]

Some commentary evidenced awareness of the idea, preached by Pearson and Kidd and demonstrated in practice by Chamberlain and Bismarck, that imperialism might salve social ills. The Reverend John Henry Barrows of Chicago said, "Some are rapidly perceiving that we are to have a better America through cherishing larger responsibilities," and Henry Watterson wrote in his *Louisville Courier-Journal:*

[7] Chicago *Times-Herald*, June 30, 1898; *Baptist Home Monthly*, XVIII (Aug. 1898), 253; Indianapolis *Journal*, July 5, 1898; Hamlin Garland, *Roadside Meetings* (New York, 1930), p. 410.

It is true that we exchange domestic dangers for foreign dangers; but in every direction we multiply the opportunities of the people. We risk Caesarism, certainly; but even Caesarism is preferable to anarchism. . . . In short, anything is better than the pace we were going when the present forces started into life.[8]

Many opponents of imperialism attacked the foreign examples and authorities that imperialists cited. The *Congregationalist* quoted Gladstone as saying, "The idea that the colonies add to the strength of the mother country appears to me to be as dark a superstition as any that existed in the Middle Ages." The Philadelphia *Public Ledger* declared:

One of the leading motives and incentives for the new American policy of expansion and adventure is that we shall thereby imitate England and improve trade, though many of the most thoughtful, knowing and eminent Englishmen of our own and other days have deprecated the British colonial policy.

Taking direct issue with Watterson, a St. Louis Presbyterian weekly said that he had "studied English politics to little purpose if he thinks England is not menaced by socialism and agrarianism. . . . Caesarism is no cure for the discontent of the masses." [9]

[8] Barrows, in a commencement address at Amherst, New York *Tribune*, June 27, 1898; Louisville *Courier-Journal*, quoted in *Literary Digest*, XVII (July 2, 1898), 3–4.

[9] *Congregationalist* and St. Louis *Observer*, quoted in *Literary Digest*, XVII (July 16, 1898), 79–80; Philadelphia *Public Ledger*, June 20, 1898.

All this rebuttal had no apparent effect. Supporters of Philippine annexation made extensive use of the example of England and words from English imperialists. The antiexpansionism of prominent men at home thus found an offset in contrary expressions from prominent men abroad, and Englishmen such as Rosebery, Chamberlain, Norman, and Kipling served as leaders of opinion for Americans.

Had the American establishment stood as solidly together as in 1869–71, words of foreigners could probably have been quoted with less effect. But in 1898 a minority of the establishment, much more impressive than the minority formed by Bennett, Ward, and a few others in 1869–71, advocated expansion.

Including such men as Olney, Lodge, Capen, Holls, Mahan, Abbott, MacArthur, Roosevelt, Tree, and Hitt, this minority seemed to represent a younger generation. Of the men just mentioned, Tree was sixty-six, Olney a little over sixty, Capen and MacArthur in their fifties, the others in their forties. A similar group of antiexpansionists, such as Carnegie, Schurz, Sigel, Godkin, Low, MacVeagh, Lincoln, and Harper, would have had an average age in the mid-sixties. The chances are that, to many, the imperialists seemed more vigorous and more forward-looking, as well as more in harmony with newer currents abroad.

In 1898 the nation's opinion leadership divided. Perhaps it would be better to say that it splintered. The imperialists pressed varying lines of argument, some emphasizing power and advantage, others duty and destiny, still others ills at home worse than those that might be flown to. They and the anti-imperialists addressed themselves to more than one issue. There resulted a cacophony in which interested citizens would sometimes have found it difficult to divine who favored expansion and who did not.

The examples of Coolidge and Reid illustrate the confusion. At the outset Coolidge's position seemed clearly anti-imperialist, and on the broad issue of whether the United States should acquire a colony, his view never wavered. On the other hand, he saw Hawaiian annexation as not necessarily contravening his principles, for he could imagine Hawaii eventually becoming sufficiently Anglo-Saxonized to qualify for entry into the union. Also, he could see acquisition of a port or even maintenance of a temporary protectorate over the Philippines as providing entrepôts to markets in Asia, continuing the westward thrust, and yielding economic advantages without leaving the United States permanently in control of a subject population. Perhaps too he could envision these limited steps postponing the triumph of communism and the day when corporate bonds ceased to have value. Coolidge's opposition to annexation of the Philippines lacked sharp definition.

Reid came out not only for taking the Philippines but, in spite of the war resolution, for retaining control of Cuba. Nevertheless his views, no less than Coolidge's, defied simple categorization. An article that Reid published in *Century* magazine in September 1898 drew a direct parallel between the position of the United States in Cuba and that of Britain in Egypt. Mooting the question of whether or not intervention in Cuba had been wise, Reid asserted that, hav-

199

ing intervened, "we made ourselves responsible for improving the situation, and . . . we cannot leave Cuba till that is done." As to the Philippines, he felt unable to present any strong argument for annexation except the absence of any alternative "consistent with our . . . honorable obligation . . . to civilization." He said candidly:

> The war is a great sorrow, and to many these results of it will seem even more mournful. They cannot be contemplated with unmixed confidence by any; and to all who think, they must be a source of some grave apprehensions. Plainly, this unwelcome war is leading us by ways we have not trod to an end we cannot surely forecast.

Reid offered some consolation. The islanders would surely benefit, he felt; construction of an interoceanic canal would come at an earlier date; and Americans could hope for "mercantile control of the Pacific Ocean." Nevertheless neither his *Century* article nor his *Tribune* editorials offered a clarion call for a colonialist movement.[10]

Some members of the establishment, to be sure, adopted simple and clear-cut stands. Charles W. Eliot helped establish the Anti-Imperialist League, which categorically opposed expansion. A number of Harvard professors joined, and so did President Rogers of Northwestern University and Von Holst of the University of Chicago. Yale's William Graham Sumner, probably the nation's best-known promoter of Social Darwinism, spoke uncompromisingly

[10] Whitelaw Reid, "The Territory with Which We Are Threatened," *Century*, XVI (Sept. 1898), 788–794.

against even temporary acquisition of Philippine territory. (In opposing imperialism, it might be added, he took the same position taken by Herbert Spencer in England.) [11]

Businessmen, lawyers, and other nonacademics seemed less disposed to approach the issue as crusaders. Though Andrew Carnegie financed the Anti-Imperialist League, Carl Schurz and Lew Wallace served it as orators and pamphleteers, and Sigmund Zeisler held office in the Chicago branch, few others who have caught our eyes in this essay played active roles in it. Its leadership came less from the foreign policy elite than from other elites usually leading campaigns for clean government or social betterment.

Similarly the establishment produced a few, but only a few, straightforward imperialists. Among them were Brooks Adams, Mahan, Judge Grosscup, and Beveridge. Perhaps one ought to add Charles A. Conant, a writer for the New York *Journal of Commerce*, Yale Professor Washburn Hopkins, a Sanskrit scholar who argued from the example of India that a "higher morality" required Anglo-Saxons to rule the lesser races, and editor St. Clair McKelway of the Brooklyn *Eagle*.[12] On the whole, how-

[11] Philip Charles Newman, "Democracy and Imperialism in American Political Thought," *Philippine Social Sciences and Humanities Review*, XV (Dec. 1950), 351–367; James P. Shenton, "Imperialism and Racism," in Donald Sheehan and Harold C. Syrett, eds., *Essays in American Historiography* (New York, 1960), pp. 231–250; Robert M. O'Neil, "The Protest Against Expansion" (manuscript in possession of the author, Berkeley, Calif.). On characteristics of the anti-imperialists, see Fred Harvey Harrington, "The Anti-Imperialist Movement in the United States, 1898–1900," *Mississippi Valley Historical Review*, XXII (Sept. 1935), 211–230.

[12] Brooks Adams, "The Commercial Future: The New Struggle for Life among Nations," *Fortnightly*, LXXI (Feb. 1899), 274–283; Alfred T.

ever, thoroughgoing imperialists and thoroughgoing anti-imperialists both came from the fringes of the establishment.

Most solid men of affairs resembled Coolidge and Reid in taking equivocal positions. Some opposed colonies but not expansion that would mean expansion of trade and influence. Many said, as did Depew, that colonies might turn out to be bad bargains, that the United States ought not to embark on an imperialist career, but that, all things considered, annexation of the Philippines seemed the most prudent course at present. This line of argument merged imperceptibly with Reid's—that the advantages of colonies *might* turn out to exceed the disadvantages.

By expressing ambivalent views, men of the establishment offered the interested public a wider range of choice than had the establishment of 1869–71. Also, they gave latitude to men who in other circumstances might have functioned merely as talkers. One can imagine a Bostonian such as James J. Myers or Edwin Ginn saying to his acquaintance, "Mr. Eliot says . . . but Mr. Coolidge says . . . and Mr. Olney says . . . ," and then producing his own reasons for siding with one or the other.

The more varied and unclear the statements from the establishment, the more widely leadership dispersed and the

Mahan, "The Relation of the United States to Their New Dependencies," *Review of Reviews,* XIX (March 1899), 335–336; Charles A. Conant, "The Struggle for Commercial Empire," *Forum,* XXVII (June 1899), 427–440; Brooklyn *Eagle,* quoted in *Literary Digest,* XVIII (Feb. 18, 1899), 185; Grosscup, quoted in *Public Opinion,* XXV (Sept. 1, 1898), 260.

more crude and ill-informed became the reasoning employed. Those predisposed toward expansion found it easier to trot out catch phrases such as "Manifest Destiny," "survival of the fittest," and "vast markets of Asia." Those predisposed against expansion could speak less qualifiedly of need to preserve racial purity, dangers created by increasing federal patronage, the army, and government spending, and perils likely to result simply from deserting the wisdom of the founding fathers. More and more, propagandists and politicians on both sides appealed, as had the expansionists of 1869–71, to an antiestablishment public.

Some who preached expansionism pretended that the Anti-Imperialist League represented the whole establishment. Among men at whom we have looked earlier, some with political ambitions adopted such a line. Holls did so. Renewing his efforts to supplant Schurz, he called the veteran leader not an American at all, but an old country liberal "à la Bamberger and Eugen Richter." Beveridge sought election to the United States Senate, denouncing anti-imperialists for "disbelief in the American people." Young comers, such as James M. Beck in Philadelphia, put similar adornments on their speeches, and men already in Washington played to the patriotism and piety of citizens who did not know the world beyond their county borders. Senator Teller of Colorado, who had been responsible for the phrases in the war resolution promising independence to Cuba, shifted stance, saying, "The American flag is capable of giving to those people American law, American freedom, American progress, and enabling them to share in prosper-

ity with us as well as in American glory." Implying that any
policy except retention of the Philippines would be sacrile-
gious, Senator Frye of Maine declared, "God opened the
door, pushed us in and closed it. No man on earth or angel
in heaven can now take us out." [13]

Anti-imperialists made equally vigorous efforts to arouse
some kind of antiestablishment public. They appealed to
class feeling. In Senate debate, Republican William E.
Mason of Illinois attributed the movement for annexing the
Philippines to a conspiracy among exporters of liquor, tobacco, and textiles and importers of sugar; Democrat
George G. Vest of Missouri blamed "the greed of the commercial and money-making classes"; and Democrat John L.
McLaurin of South Carolina, "the trusts and the money
power . . . crying out for new fields to exploit." The
antiannexation bloc loudly claimed to represent American
rather than foreign principles. Mason accused McKinley of
imitating English rulers, and Democratic Senator Augustus
O. Bacon of Georgia spoke of the administration's moving
into the Far East "in order that England may carry out her
schemes of foreign colonization and foreign dominion."
Even members of the Anti-Imperialist League made use of
this charge. A league pamphlet said, "Never was a nation so
lucky as England in finding the paws of a mighty cat to put
in the fire in place of her own," and so aristocratic a league

[13] For Holls, see Alfred Vagts, *Deutschland und die Vereinigten
Staaten in der Weltpolitik*, 2 vols. (New York, 1935), II, 589–590; also
see Claude G. Bowers, *Beveridge and the Progressive Era* (Boston, 1932),
p. 73; Morton Keller, *In Defense of Yesterday: James M. Beck and the
Politics of Conservatism* (New York, 1958), 53–55; Teller, in 55 Cong.,
3 sess., *Congressional Record*, p. 327; Frye, quoted in *Literary Digest*,
XIX (Aug. 19, 1899), 213.

member as Charles Francis Adams wrote, "Instead of finding our precedents in the experience of England or any
other European power, I would suggest that the true course
for this country . . . is exactly the course we have hereto-
fore pursued." [14]

While courting a public assumed to be hostile to the establishment, imperialist and anti-imperialist politicians sought
also to appeal to the establishment. Senators Platt of
Connecticut and Foraker of Ohio, both given to demagoguery on other issues, showed great restraint when advocating annexation of the Philippines. Both delivered legalis-
tic addresses, full of quotations and citations, arguing that
the founding fathers and subsequent interpreters of the
Constitution had envisioned the possibility of the nation's
acquiring and holding colonies. On the other side, Senator
Donelson Caffery of Louisiana argued against taking the
Philippines, quoting extensively from Seeley and Kidd to
support a contention that Anglo-Saxons did not flourish in
the tropics.[15]

The administration, having decided to annex the Philippines, employed successfully the tactic with which Grant
had failed in 1870. McKinley appointed a commission to
survey conditions in the islands. To head it he chose an establishment man known to hold antiannexationist views.
Imitating Grant to the letter, McKinley selected Andrew
D. White's successor at Cornell University, Jacob Gould
Schurman. Earlier, just after the Philippine issue had arisen,

[14] 55 Cong., 3 sess., *Congressional Record*, pp. 96, 528–534, 562–563, 638–
642, 733–739; Morrison I. Swift, *Imperialism and Liberty* (n.p., n.d.);
Adams quoted in *Literary Digest*, XVIII (Jan. 7, 1899), 2.
[15] 55 Cong., 3 sess., *Congressional Record*, pp. 287–297, 438–439, 563–572.

the President had named as Secretary of State John Hay, a close friend not only of Lodge, Theodore Roosevelt, and their set but also of Reid, Whitney, and others in the New York establishment. With the peace treaty awaiting ratification, McKinley appointed Columbia law professor David Jayne Hill as Hay's deputy and Joseph H. Choate as ambassador to Great Britain. Coupled with official denials that ratification of the treaty would necessarily determine whether the United States kept the Philippines or eventually made them independent, these moves helped to preserve divisions and an appearance of uncertainty within the establishment. Probably, too, they helped to prevent an antiestablishment public from taking clear form as a force either for or against imperialism.

With the foreign policy elite at sixes and sevens and a much larger public taking interest in the question of whether or not to expand, the McKinley administration succeeded in doing what the Grant administration had failed to do. By using a variety of pressures, it rallied to the treaty all but two of the doubtful Republicans in the Senate. For reasons of his own, Bryan recommended that Democrats not use the two-thirds rule to block action desired by a Senate majority. As a result, the treaty with Spain, ceding the United States title to the Philippines, passed with one vote to spare.[16]

Defeat of the Dominican treaty twenty-nine years earlier

[16] Leech, *In the Days of McKinley*, pp. 354–358; Morgan, *McKinley and His America*, pp. 414–422; Paolo E. Coletta, "Bryan, McKinley, and the Treaty of Paris," *Pacific Historical Review*, XXVI (May 1957), 131–146.

had been read as an oracular national decision against expansion. Defeat of the Versailles Treaty twenty years later was to be interpreted as a binding popular verdict against collective-security arrangements. According to the custom that these two instances illustrate, the two-thirds vote in favor of annexing the Philippines should have established colonial imperialism as a new American tradition.

For a time it seemed as if this would be so. Though having denied it earlier, the President began to say that the treaty gave the United States a Philippine colony and that only a positive decree to the contrary by Congress would change the situation. Schurman came back from the islands asserting that the United States would have to remain indefinitely. Meanwhile Reid, speaking as an intimate of the President, employed much more imperialistic language than earlier. To acquire the Philippines, he said, was "to fence in the China Sea and secure [a] . . . commanding position on the other side of the Pacific—doubling our control of it and of the fabulous trade the twentieth century will see it bear." To have done otherwise, he declared, would have been to yield to "a mushy sentimentality . . . alike un-American and un-Christian." Hinting of possible future moves, Assistant Secretary of State Hill urged in the *Forum* that American policy be thought of not as expansion or imperialism but as "the extension of civilization." [17]

[17] *Speeches and Addresses of William McKinley from March 1, 1897, to May 30, 1900* (New York, 1900), pp. 185–192; Jacob G. Schurman, *Our Duty in the Philippines* (n.p., n.d.); speech by Reid, quoted in *Literary Digest*, XVIII (Feb. 25, 1899), 211–213; David J. Hill, "The War and the Extension of Civilization," *Forum*, XXVI, (Feb. 1899), 650–655.

Such a view became more and more widely held. Though Bryan and Cleveland continued to criticize the decision to annex the Philippines, many Democrats and Democratic organs, especially those unenthusiastic about Bryan, turned toward a different position. New York financier Perry Belmont, Tammany chief Richard Croker, and former governor and senator John M. Palmer of Illinois said the United States had probably acted rightly in retaining the Philippines. Editorials in the Philadelphia *Record*, the Atlanta *Constitution*, and the New Orleans *Times-Picayune* expressed a similar judgment. Local election returns in November 1899 seemed even to the stoutly antiexpansionist New York *Evening Post* and New York *World* "a victory for imperialism." [18]

Meanwhile discussion turned to new possibilities for expansion. In late August 1899 the *Literary Digest* observed:

> Considerable change in public sentiment has appeared during the last few months with regard to Cuba's future government, and where a year and a half ago the American press was almost unanimous in calling for Cuban independence, there is now a strong undercurrent of opinion in favor of annexation.

In the autumn this undercurrent gained force. The Boston *Herald*, the New York *Journal of Commerce*, the Chicago *Inter-Ocean*, and dailies in Ohio, Minnesota, Missouri, Texas, South Dakota, and Oregon came out for reversal of

[18] *Literary Digest*, XVIII (April 1, 1899), 363–364; *ibid.*, XIX (Nov. 18, 1899), 603.

the promise of independence. Kohlsaat's Chicago *Times-Herald* asserted that "annexation would be a blessing." Though McKinley did not commit himself, he said in December 1899 that Cuban independence should not be "a hasty experiment." [19]

Early in 1900 rumors circulated of secret negotiations reviving the project for purchase of the Danish West Indies. Applauding the report, Reid's New York *Tribune* remarked, "It will be a blessing to the islands if they come under our flag, and we can make them worth much more to the country than their cost." [20]

At almost the same time dispatches from the Far East told of antiforeign violence in China and of new moves in European capitals foreshadowing that country's partitioning. The Boston *Herald* said editorially that the United States would have no choice but to take part in determining China's "future political and trade status," and the New York *Journal of Commerce* declared that the Chinese would "have . . . to establish a civilized government . . . or have one established over them." Coincidentally, books appeared by Brooks Adams, Charles A. Conant, and Josiah Strong, all forecasting ultimate American dominion over most of the Pacific and East Asia. Many signs suggested that the events of 1898–99 merely marked the beginning of America's career as a colonial power.[21]

---

[19] *Literary Digest*, XIX (Aug. 26, 1899), 245–246; David F. Healy, *The United States in Cuba, 1898–1902: Generals, Politicians and the Search for Policy* (Madison, Wis., 1963), pp. 120–123.
[20] *Literary Digest*, XX (Jan. 13, 1900), 389.
[21] *Literary Digest*, XX (Jan. 13, 1900), 35–36, (April 7, 1900), 415–416; *ibid.*, XXI (July 7, 1900), 2–3; (July 21, 1900), 62; (Aug. 4, 1900), 123–

Then the current shifted. Bryan, whose strength among Democratic state and local committees ensured him a second try at the presidency, indicated that he would make criticism of the administration's imperialism an important part of his campaign. Theretofore the play he meant to give this issue had remained uncertain. The Nebraska State Democratic platform, drafted in part by him, had called for eventual Philippine independence, but laid much more emphasis on demands for free coinage of silver and curbing of trusts. Only as convention time approached did Bryan reveal his intention. When he did, Democrats who had disagreed with him about the Philippines changed front, with Croker promising Tammany's support for an anti-imperialist campaign and Olney publishing in the *Atlantic* a jesuitical article saying that the American empire should include Cuba but not possessions in the Far East. The national party platform then named imperialism as the foremost issue, and Bryan, as the nominee, devoted his initial efforts to wooing the Anti-Imperialist League and Schurz's following among German-Americans.[22]

As if fearful that the Democrats had found a winning issue, the administration gave loud publicity to Secretary

---

124; *Public Opinion*, XXVIII (June 21, 1900), 772–774; Brooks Adams, *America's Economic Supremacy* (New York, 1900); Charles A. Conant, *The United States in the Orient* (Boston and New York, 1900); Josiah Strong, *Expansion under New World Conditions* (New York, 1900).

22 *Literary Digest*, XX (March 31, 1900), 388–389; *ibid.*, XXI (July 21, 1900), 64; (Aug. 25, 1900), 215–217; (Sept. 15, 1900), 303–304; J. Rogers Hollingsworth, *The Whirligig of Politics: The Democracy of Cleveland and Bryan* (Chicago, 1963), pp. 173–175; William J. Bryan, *The Second Battle* (Chicago, 1900).

Hay's circular requesting that the powers preserve an open door for trade in China, claiming that the United States thus expressed its opposition to imperialism. Several newspapers classifying themselves as anti-imperialist, among them the Boston *Evening Transcript*, the New York *Herald*, and the New York *Evening Post*, commended McKinley and Hay for coming back toward a proper view of America's world role. Confronted with further violence in China and a rupture of communications with legations in Peking, the administration announced that it would contribute units to an international expeditionary force. At the same time, however, Hay informed the press that he had dispatched a second note, defining America's aim as the preservation of Chinese territorial and administrative integrity. This action too drew praise from anti-imperialist papers, and Republican organs close to McKinley portrayed it as proving the administration not to be imperialistic.[23]

After McKinley's renomination the White House announced that Cuban independence could be expected shortly. The three newspapers regarded as administration organs, Reid's *Tribune*, Postmaster General Charles Emory Smith's Philadelphia *Press*, and Kohlsaat's Chicago *Times-Herald*, all published editorials describing this announcement as further discrediting opposition efforts to tag the President as an imperialist. During the campaign both Mc-

---

[23] *Literary Digest*, XXI (July 21, 1900), 62; (Sept. 1, 1900), 241; *Public Opinion*, XXIX (July 5, 1900), 8-9; (July 19, 1900), 73; Marilyn B. Young, "American China Policy, 1895-1901," unpubl. diss. (Harvard, 1963).

Kinley and vice-presidential nominee Theodore Roosevelt denied plans for further territorial acquisitions. The administration, they conceded, believed in expansion, but only in the expansion of American trade and influence.[24]

McKinley won endorsement from men who had opposed annexation of the Philippines. Though Schurz backed Bryan, Carnegie and Abram S. Hewitt came out for the President. So did Wayne MacVeagh, who said he was satisfied that McKinley's reelection would mean the nation's "return to its true mission, that of developing the rich and great American continent and dedicating it to liberty and peace." The "present tendency of President McKinley's mind," MacVeagh went on, "can be discerned in the true American policy he is now pursuing in China."[25]

Politicians judged the public to have lost enthusiasm for empire. Senator Cushman K. Davis of Minnesota wrote regretfully to Reid that "the transient people . . . have never believed in or understood the 'swelling act of the imperial theme.'" Platt of Connecticut, who still hoped the United States might keep Cuba, warned General Leonard Wood, "The whole Congress is nervous, liable to take the bit in its teeth and say we ought to get out of Cuba."[26]

Nor did professionals change their minds because of McKinley's reelection. No one remembering his campaign or

[24] *Literary Digest*, XXI (Aug. 4, 1900), 126–127; *ibid.*, XXII (Feb. 16, 1901), 181–182; Thomas A. Bailey, "Was the Election of 1900 a Mandate on Imperialism?," *Mississippi Valley Historical Review*, XXIV (June 1937), 43–52.

[25] *Literary Digest*, XXI (Oct. 20, 1900), 453.

[26] Cortissoz, *Reid*, II, 265; Healy, *The United States in Cuba*, 142.

SOME TENTATIVE EXPLANATION

Roosevelt's could interpret the Republican victory as a triumph for imperialism. Administration organs did not do so, and McKinley made no return to "the imperial theme" after being assured another term. In fact he moved almost at once, through the Platt Amendment, to give Cuba at least nominally its promised independence.

In the autumn of 1901, to be sure, the administration concluded a treaty for purchase of the Danish West Indies. But since negotiations had opened more than a year earlier, this treaty constituted a carry-over from the past. Taking it up early in 1902, after McKinley's assassination, the Senate handled it as a legacy from a martyred President and ratified with little debate. On the whole, the press eschewed comment. When the Danish Rigsdag then turned the treaty down, few expressed regret. The *Literary Digest* quoted as a typical newspaper reaction the comment of the Pittsburgh *Gazette:* "The United States has worried along without the Danish islands until this time, and can continue to do so." [27]

Once in a while came an echo of "the imperial theme" of 1898–99. When Panama seceded from Colombia and leased a canal zone to the United States, one or two newspapers mentioned the possibility of making Panama itself a colony. St. Clair McKelway continued in the Brooklyn *Eagle* to advocate annexation of Cuba and other Caribbean islands. Henry King, the editor of the St. Louis *Globe-Democrat,* campaigned for colonizing Haiti and the Dominican Republic. Theirs were, however, isolated voices.[28]

[27] *Literary Digest,* XXV (Nov. 1, 1902), 543–544.
[28] *Literary Digest,* XXIV (April 5, 1902), 456; (May 31, 1902), 733;

In 1904–1905 a real possibility presented itself, for the first time in over thirty years, of annexing the Dominican Republic. Divided into warring factions and pressed by both American and European creditors, Dominican political leaders invited the United States to assume some kind of control over the country's affairs. When rumors spread that Roosevelt would agree to American supervision of Dominican finances even the loyal New York *Tribune* commented, "That is a good deal to ask." When the rumor proved true and Roosevelt presented the agreement to the Senate, Republicans as well as Democrats blocked its ratification. The President had to settle, at least temporarily, for an unratified *modus vivendi*. Neither senators nor newspaper editors exhibited appetite for a Dominican colony. Roosevelt himself commented, "I have about the same desire to annex it as a gorged boa-constrictor might have to swallow a porcupine wrong-end-to." [29]

By that time Republican leaders had begun to voice doubts even about the Philippines. On Memorial Day, 1902, Roosevelt had spoken of possible eventual independence for the islands. His words enabled onetime anti-imperialist dailies to say that a difference in principle no longer separated the administration from its former critics and that the only

---

ibid., XXV (Sept. 20, 1902), 340; *ibid.*, XXVIII (March 5, 1904), 319. And even the *Globe-Democrat* had changed its tune by 1905, when it questioned the wisdom of assuming control over Dominican finances (*ibid.*, XXX [March 18, 1905], 387).

[29] *Literary Digest*, XXX (Jan. 28, 1905), 120; (Feb. 4, 1905), 157; (March 25, 1905), 419–420; Morison, *Letters of Theodore Roosevelt*, IV, 734.

remaining difference concerned timing. In 1904 Elihu Root, after leaving the Secretaryship of War, prophesied that the Philippines would eventually go the way of Cuba.[30]

In 1898 the imperialist movement had been powerful, and the Senate's vote to annex the Philippines provided a starting point for a new consensus favorable to future colonial expansion. For about a year afterward such a consensus seemed in the making, foreshadowing a time when Hawaii and the Philippines would stand as merely the first members of a vast and growing colonial empire. During 1900 the new current slowed and stopped. Before long, majority opinion once again ran in the old channel. Dismissing the possibility of further colonial expansion, Lodge commented in 1903, "The American people have lost all interest in it." [31] How does one explain this reversal?

Simple lapse of time accounts for much. Without dramatic incidents to hold their attention, the members of Senator Davis' "transient public" lost interest. The possibility of their becoming engaged once again with the subject diminished as the issues became more complicated. Could tariffs be imposed on imports from the new possessions, or would the Constitution compel free entry of sugar, tobacco, and other products harvested by cheap colonial labor? Would Congress have to require that imports into the colonies pay the same tariffs as imports received on the continent? If so, the colonists would be denied cheap prod-

[30] *Literary Digest*, XXIV (June 14, 1902), 791–792; *ibid.*, XXVIII (Feb. 13, 1904), 208.

[31] John A. Garraty, *Henry Cabot Lodge, A Biography* (New York, 1953), p. 210.

ucts from nearby lands. If not, the colonists could import goods, reexport them to the mainland, and conceivably subvert the protective system. These issues did not make their way to the decision docket of the Supreme Court until after the 1900 election. As Mr. Dooley remarked,

> Th' men that argyied that th' Constitution ought to shadow th' flag to all th' tough resorts on th' Passyfic coast an' th' men that argyied that th' flag was so lively that no Constitution cud follow it an' survive, they died or lost their jobs or wint back to Salem an' wer' f'rgotten. Expansionists contracted an' anti-expansionists blew up, an' little childher was born into th' wurruld an' grew to manhood an' niver heerd in Pother Ricky except whin some wan got a job there.[32]

During the interval many deep-dyed protectionists probably lost enthusiasm for colonies.

As the interested public shrank, its composition changed. Though containing some convinced imperialists, this smaller public also contained active members of the Anti-Imperialist League and, perhaps more important, men who felt their personal interests jeopardized by colonial expansion: cane and sugar-beet growers and producers of tobacco fearing competition from tropical colonies; Irish-Americans seeing that imperialism promoted Anglo-American solidarity, reduced sympathy for the Irish cause, and weakened Irish power in American politics; and German-

[32] *Literary Digest*, XXII (June 22, 1901), 751.

Americans who, for similar reasons, regretted any tightening of American ties with England and feared, in addition, increasing friction with their own aggressively expanding fatherland. When back to normal dimensions, the interested public probably possessed a large anti-imperialist component.

And some who applauded expansion in 1898–99 changed their minds as a result of the Philippine insurrection.[33] At almost the moment when the Senate approved annexation of the islands, Filipinos led by Emilio Aguinaldo opened a war for independence. Employing guerilla tactics, they eluded and harassed American forces, engaging a large part of the regular army and requiring that some wartime volunteers remain in service. Numbers of American troops fighting the guerillas grew from 30,000 in 1899 to 60,000 in 1900, with little or no evidence of headway toward pacification.

Impatient congressmen and newspaper editors called for expanding the American force to 100,000 and replacing the generals in command. Despite the approach of the election, staunch Republican papers took the President to task for his failure to bring the war to an end. Later, as reports filtered back that captives had been tortured for information, potential rebel supporters had been herded into concentration camps, and troops had been sent into one pro-rebel area with orders to make it a "howling wilderness," some of the same

[33] Leon Wolff, *Little Brown Brother* (Garden City, N. Y., 1961), gives the best account of the early days of American occupation in the Philippines.

2 1 7

papers criticized the administration for tolerating such inhumanity.[34]

Anti-imperialists capitalized on discontent caused by the war, and onetime imperialists confessed chagrin at Filipino resistance to the blessings of liberty. Fear that the same kind of war might erupt in Cuba clearly had some quieting effect on ardor for annexation, especially since the army had no troops with which to fight it; and the fact that severe fighting continued in the Philippines until well into 1901 must have had an effect on all thought of possible new extensions of empire. Probably, in fact, it was the Philippine insurrection more than anything else that quelled any nascent imperialist movement.

The coincidental war between Britain and the Boer republics, which had far-reaching effects on ideas about empire within the international liberal community, was not without some impact on American thought. Opening in mid-October 1899, this war saw Britain suffer a series of humiliating defeats. It ended in a British victory, but only after hard campaigning, running into 1902, and after Britain had committed 300,000 troops to cope with an enemy numbering no more than 75,000. Watching its grim course, many Englishmen and Europeans lost their romantic ideas about imperialism.

Some so affected had friends in America. Within a month after the war's opening Cecil Spring Rice wrote Mrs. Theodore Roosevelt of having "*doubts* of all kinds which are

[34] *Literary Digest*, XIX (July 8, 1899), 32; Leech, *In the Days of McKinley*, pp. 357–365, 397–409.

most horrible." [35] William T. Stead, the editor of the *Pall Mall Gazette*, testified publicly to experiencing a complete change of mind about imperialism. Previously a trumpeter of England's holy imperial mission, he had visited the United States, written best sellers about crime and Christianity in Chicago and New York, and been a patron of Chicago's Columbian Exhibition. One of those crusaders against immorality whose lectures and writings combined righteousness with spiciness, he drew many American listeners and readers. When he suddenly turned against imperialism, Kohlsaat's Chicago *Times-Herald* and other American periodicals publicized the event.[36]

Day in and day out the American press also reported the powerful reaction in England within the Liberal party against Rosebery and other imperialists. Those who clung to the label "Liberal Imperialist" merely supported the war, while many others came out in open opposition, among them the party's younger, more dashing, and more imaginative leaders. By 1901 few men in English politics who commanded admiration in America still voiced the expansionist zest of the previous decade, and liberals on the continent seemed unanimous not only in decrying British imperialism but in turning away from colonialist movements in their own countries.[37]

[35] Gwynn, *Spring Rice*, I, 300.

[36] Frederic Whyte, *The Life of W. T. Stead*, 2 vols. (London, 1925), I, 174.

[37] See Koebner, *Imperialism*, pp. 221–236, 243–249; Elié Halévy, *History of the English People*, 2nd rev. ed. (London, 1951), V (*Imperialism and the Rise of Labour, 1895–1905*), pp. 93–110; and Semmel, *Imperialism and Social Reform*, pp. 59–64; E. Malcolm Carroll, *French Public Opinion*

A new anti-imperialist doctrine quite different from that of Cobden and Bright meanwhile caught the fancy of liberal intellectuals in England and elsewhere. Best represented by John A. Hobson's *Imperialism*, this doctrine held colonies to be of benefit primarily to capitalists.[38] With abundant statistics Hobson showed colonial trade to yield little for either producers or shippers. Capitalists, on the other hand, could no longer find sufficiently profitable uses at home for the large profits they earned, Hobson contended, and they therefore needed to reach into primitive lands for new opportunities to place funds in railroads, factories, and the like. Since their funds could not be safe if natives remained in charge, they wanted their own governments in control. Then they could net handsome returns.

These theses appealed to Englishmen who saw the contest in South Africa as at base a war to defend the property of Cecil Rhodes and other English and German-English in-

---

and *Foreign Affairs, 1870–1914* (New York, 1931), pp. 180–181; Brunschwig, *French Colonialism*, pp. 135–181.

[38] John A. Hobson's *Imperialism* (London, 1902) is the best known, most systematic, and most important presentation of the case, but it was not immediately the most influential. Americans came to know Hobson's theory first through his *The War in South Africa: Its Causes and Effects* (New York, 1900), which sold well and was enthusiastically reviewed, as in, e.g., *Nation*, LXX (April 12, 1900), 285–286; *Outlook*, LXIV (April 7, 1900), 840; *Independent*, LII (April 5, 1900), 835; and *Atlantic*, LXXXVII (Jan. 1901), 55–56. *Imperialism*, which was published in an American edition late in 1902, was scarcely noticed at first. The only American journals in which I could locate reviews were the *Quarterly Journal of Economics*, XVII (Feb. 1903), 355, and the *Journal of Political Economy*, XI (March 1903), 311–315. Still, it is fair to say, because of the earlier book and the pirating of Hobson's theses by editors such as Stead, that the doctrines of *Imperialism* were in circulation.

vestors. Many saw it thus, among them Spring Rice and Stead.[39] And Americans already disillusioned by the Philippine war and concerned about the growing power of trusts probably found Hobson's arguments especially attractive. They could return to anticolonialism while remaining in tune with the most up-to-date thought abroad.

The complexities of the colonial issue, the Philippine insurrection, the Boer War, and the turn in foreign liberal opinion combined to have a powerful effect on members of the American establishment. Olney remarked shamefacedly that he had been "a little dazzled by our new possessions." Lyman Abbott, who published a strongly imperialist article during the campaign of 1900, confessed within a year that the Boer War had altered his opinion. Albert Shaw went through a similar change. In 1902 he counseled his friend Beveridge against saying that the United States would "never" withdraw from the Philippines.[40]

Theodore Roosevelt's letters showed a similar pattern.[41] In December 1899 he rebuked Spring Rice for signs of disillusionment. "I believe in the expansion of great nations," he wrote. "India has done an incalculable amount for the English character. If we do our work well in the Philippines and

[39] Gwynn, *Spring Rice*, I, 301; Whyte, *Stead*, II, 167–168. See W. T. Stead, "The True Imperialism," *Review of Reviews*, XXI (May 15, 1900), 441–449.

[40] Olney to S. B. Griffin, Feb. 5, 1900, Private Papers of Richard Olney, Library of Congress; Ira V. Brown, *Lyman Abbott, Christian Evolutionist: A Study in Religious Liberalism* (Cambridge, Mass., 1953), pp. 171–172; Bowers, *Beveridge*, pp. 176–177.

[41] The following quotations are from Morison, *Letters of Theodore Roosevelt*, II, 1104, 1233, 1270, 1415.

the West Indies, it will do a great deal for our character." A few months later he commented on his agreement with the *Spectator's* "disapproval of Cecil Rhodes and the capitalist gang." He also mused that the English-speaking races might have become too citified to be effective colonizers.

"The more I have looked into the Boer War," Roosevelt wrote in April 1900, "the more uncomfortable I have felt about it." Hearing of agitation in favor of America's seizing a base in the Levant, he wrote the Secretary of War opposing such a step. The United States, he warned, might find itself in worse plight than Britain in South Africa.

Though he continued to defend the decision to annex the Philippines, Roosevelt gave evidence quite early of a change of heart. Soon after the election he wrote in a private letter, "Whenever the [Philippine] islands can stand alone, I shall be only too glad to withdraw." Addressed to President Eliot of Harvard, this letter may have been insincere. Nevertheless Roosevelt showed himself much cooler than before toward projects for Cuban annexation and, in fact, never again displayed zeal for acquisition of a colony.

Not all onetime imperialists made such a quick transition. Mahan, Holls, and Beveridge continued to speak favorably of colonies long after doing so had ceased to be fashionable.[42] As early as 1902 or 1903, however, they formed as small a minority as Bennett and Ward had formed in the 1870s. The American establishment once again pos-

---

[42] W. D. Puleston, *Mahan* (New Haven, 1934), pp. 220–229; Vagts, *Deutschland und die Vereinigten Staaten*, II, 1509, 1575, 1971–1972; Bowers, *Beveridge*, pp. 176–177.

sessed an anticolonial consensus as firm as that which had existed in the early 1880s.

In all likelihood this fact had something to do with the shrinkage of the interested public. Had the establishment remained as divided and confused as in 1898–99, less well qualified men might have continued to figure as leaders of opinion. As it was, the words of the latter on such questions as whether or not to retain Cuba or annex the Danish West Indies and the Dominican Republic ceased to be solicited by politicians or featured in the press. Establishment men predominated in presidential and senatorial correspondence and columns of daily newspapers relating to foreign policy. Speaking again with a common voice, the establishment said clearly that tradition, economic interest, domestic conditions, and the teachings of social science all argued against colonialism.

If accurate, this description of what happened between 1898 and 1902 or 1903 has implications running beyond the subject of this essay. One is that the public interested in a given issue may vary in size according not only to the issue but also to the character of its leadership. If the establishment had been as much of one mind in 1898 as earlier and later, the Philippines might have stirred no livelier concern than Hawaii in 1893 or the Dominican Republic in 1904–1905. A high level of public interest in any question may be due no more to the importance of the question than to the presence of discord and confusion among men to whom interested citizens look for guidance.

The quality of public opinion about an issue may also

223

depend on the clarity with which conspicuous opinion leaders express their views. In this instance emotionalism increased dramatically as leadership dispersed to men who ordinarily deferred to the establishment. Perhaps a similar loosening of customary restraints accounted in part for the Red scares of 1919 and the early 1950s. As lawyers and community leaders betrayed confusion, others took it on themselves to propose means of dealing with Communist espionage and subversion, opportunities for demagoguery arose, and politicians appealed successfully to antiestablishment publics. Certainly, as Samuel Stouffer's surveys discovered, a wide gap existed in the mid-1950s between views circulating in leadership groups and views regarded by politicians as those of the interested public.[43] Conceivably some-

[43] Samuel A. Stouffer, *Communism, Conformity,* and *Civil Liberties* (New York, 1955). The assumption that establishment opinion is relatively wise is, of course, open to challenge. Sidney E. Verba, "Assumptions of Rationality and Non-Rationality in Models of the International System," *World Politics,* XIV (Oct. 1961), 92–114, suggests that the greater an individual's interest in a given issue, the more likely is his opinion to be a function of his personality and hence, perhaps, of his anxieties and neuroses. William A. Gamson and André Modigliani, "Knowledge and Foreign Policy Opinions: Some Models for Consideration," *Public Opinion Quarterly,* XXX (Summer 1966), 187–199, raise questions as to whether greater knowledge of or better understanding of an issue does more than fix an individual in beliefs toward which he is psychically disposed. On the other hand, there is psychometric data supporting the more common-sense supposition that a relationship exists between, on the one hand, an individual's intelligence, education, and information on a given subject and, on the other hand, his sense of its complexities, his discrimination among the issues involved, and his capacity to change his mind. See Carl I. Hovland, Irving L. Janis, and Harold H. Kelley, *Communications and Persuasion* (New Haven, 1953), pp. 181–204; Hovland and Janis, *Personality and Persuasibility* (New Haven, 1951), *passim;* Milton J. Rosenberg *et al., Attitude Organization and Change: An Analysis of Consistency among Attitude Components* (New Haven, 1960); Herbert C.

thing similar could occur if the foreign policy establishment should at some point display confusion and discord about preemptive nuclear warfare. Further study of how elites shape effective public opinion thus may have other uses besides illumination of the past.

Since this essay deals with a unique moment, its generalizations do not necessarily carry far forward or far backward in time. The late nineteenth-century United States had just begun to become a complex of interdependent cities and industrial centers. Its national government had limited functions, among which the conduct of foreign relations had only newly acquired fresh importance. Congress played a large but ill-defined role in determining policy, and, for both the executive and legislative branches, methods of measuring and influencing opinion remained crude. In consequence, politicians may have gauged public views in the unfamiliar area of foreign policy by observing a small cosmopolitan elite. Earlier, when the nation had a different character, they may have made more use of other measurements. Later, when the federal machine had grown and new techniques of communication, persuasion, and opinion measurement had developed, they may have used still others. Though the suggestions offered in this essay ought to be investigated in other contexts, they remain only suggestions.

Kelman, "Processes of Opinion Change," *Public Opinion Quarterly*, XXV (Spring 1961), 57–78; and Nathan Maccoby and Eleanor E. Maccoby, "Homeostatic Theory in Attitude Change," *Public Opinion Quarterly*, XXV (Winter 1961), 538–545.

Primarily the object of this essay is to set forth a synthetic interpretation of a single episode. Trying to take account of the easily forgotten fact that public opinion is seldom if ever opinion among more than an interested minority of the electorate, it has emphasized the small group of opinion leaders that gave this minority some guidance and, perhaps more importantly, provided political leaders with evidence as to how the interested public might bend.

Though these opinion leaders seemed for an interval not to be directing or representing the public, that interval was short. Most of the time the men whom we have described as members of the foreign policy establishment served as the voices of effective opinion, and their expressed views underwent changes. Through the 1870s and 1880s they opposed America's acquiring colonies. By 1893 they had adopted a different outlook and, by and large, approved of annexing Hawaii. Only from the outbreak of the Spanish war in 1898 to some point in 1900 or 1901 did they not either concur or divide along clear lines corresponding to party lines. After 1901 they agreed once again that the United States did not need and should not want colonial possessions.

Forces that various historians have singled out account in large part for these shifts in opinion. A sense of the nation's varied traditions clearly had great importance. Few members of the establishment could even momentarily have approved colonial expansion if they had not remembered Louisiana, Florida, the Mexican cession, and Alaska, and expansionist utterances by Jefferson, Jackson, Polk, and Sew-

226

ard. These men did not necessarily choose the tradition of Manifest Destiny while discarding the tradition of Mission, for many who spoke for annexation of Hawaii, the Philippines, or other territories claimed to be arguing for the nation's self-fulfillment as a propagator of liberty, democracy, and progress. Accepted meanings of American traditions changed during these years. Even so, these traditions had much to do with shaping men's convictions.

Economic considerations had at least equal importance. The apparent needs of American business concerned most men in the foreign policy establishment. Few could have inclined to imperialism without believing that colonies would make the country more prosperous. Equally, however, few could have opposed imperialism except from conviction that the benefits would be meager and, in the long run, well below the costs.

All men in the establishment could see evidence of increasing productive capacity and lagging domestic consumption. Apprehensive about future internal growth and aware of European economic nationalism, all must have hoped that the millions in underdeveloped lands would become customers for American products. Adding these factors up, however, individuals arrived at different sums. Like tradition, economic logic led to no single, ineluctable conclusion, nor did Social Darwinism or the "psychic crisis."

While Social Darwinist phrases probably influenced some men in the establishment, they constituted less of a constraint than either history or economics. Certain courses of action could not be rationalized by reference to Manifest

Destiny or Mission or need for new markets, but almost any course could be justified as part of a "struggle for survival." Witness the fact that extremists on both sides used this argument. Similarly, almost any action could be defended as necessary to appease or avoid exciting an irrational public. Social Darwinism and the "psychic crisis" would have colored thought but not determined the positions men took on the colonial issue.

International fashions in thought and events on the world scene could have had a decisive influence on men of the establishment.[44] Not that they attached more importance to keeping step with Europeans than to preserving tradition, furthering trade, obeying scientific laws, or preventing domestic upheaval. Quite the contrary. But knowledge of foreign thought affected their ideas about America's world mission and their understanding of Social Darwinism. Observation of foreign experience suggested to them alternative methods of promoting national prosperity and dealing with

[44] That this was not the case exclusively with the foreign policy establishment is demonstrated in Arthur Mann, "British Social Thought and American Reformers of the Progressive Era," *Mississippi Valley Historical Review*, XLII (March 1956), 672–692. The interplay of opinion movements in America, England, and Europe needs very much to be investigated, most obviously in relation to protectionism, economic nationalism, and social welfare legislation; and a factor to be taken into account, here as well as in connection with foreign policy, is the role of foreign reference groups and "reference idols." To what extent was American progressivism influenced by observation of Germany's experiments or by tendencies within the English Liberal party? To what extent in turn were Germans and Englishmen affected by what they saw of American progressivism and liberalism, as symbolized by Theodore Roosevelt and Woodrow Wilson? In what degree was cosmopolitanism or lack thereof, or differences in foreign reference groups, a cause of division within reform movements on both sides of the Atlantic?

social discontent. Above all, the foreign scene provided models for imitation (reference groups and reference idols, in social science jargon). The well-traveled and well-read American could select a position on the colonial issue by identifying it with, on the one hand, Bright, Gladstone, Morley, and Richter or, on the other, Rosebery, Chamberlain, Ferry, Bismarck, or Wilhelm II. Neither the American past nor an assessment of American economic needs nor Social Darwinism nor the domestic political scene offered such guidance.

Men of the establishment belonged both to their own country and to a larger Atlantic community. Ordinarily they defined opinion for an interested public, most of whom had less familiarity with currents abroad. Probably this fact explains in part why, when the establishment ceased to be coherent and leadership dispersed, apparent public opinion on colonies became so simplistic and emotional. It may also explain why, when the interested public appeared to be expanding, many politicians took an antiestablishment tack: they realized that a gulf separated the citizen of the Atlantic community from the citizen whose outlook comprehended only his county or state. Currents running within the larger community help to account for American public opinion not so much because they influenced a large number of Americans as because they influenced the few who set styles within a normally small foreign policy public.

As stated in the beginning, this essay does not dispute what other historians have said. On the contrary, it seeks to

229

draw together previous interpretations by means of hypotheses about late nineteenth-century public opinion, its manifestations, and the play within it of tradition, economic interest, Social Darwinism, and psychological malaise, together with awareness of ideas and events abroad. I hope others will advance alternative hypotheses, for my aim is not to close debate but rather to reopen it by prompting new questions about this and other episodes. In the literal meaning of the term, this work is an essay.

INDEX

ERNEST R. MAY

A professor of history, an officer of the Institute of Politics in the John F. Kennedy School of Government, and a member of the administrative committee of the Charles Warren Center for the Study of American History at Harvard University, Ernest R. May teaches and directs research on international politics and American foreign policy in the twentieth century. His previous books include *Imperial Democracy: The Emergence of America as a Great Power* (1961) and *The World War and American Isolation, 1914–1917* (1959), as well as a much discussed American history textbook for junior high schools, *Land of the Free*, co-authored with John W. Caughey and John Hope Franklin.

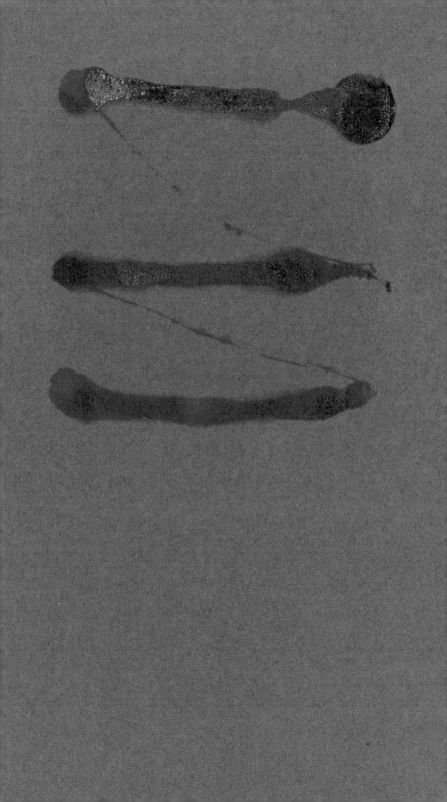

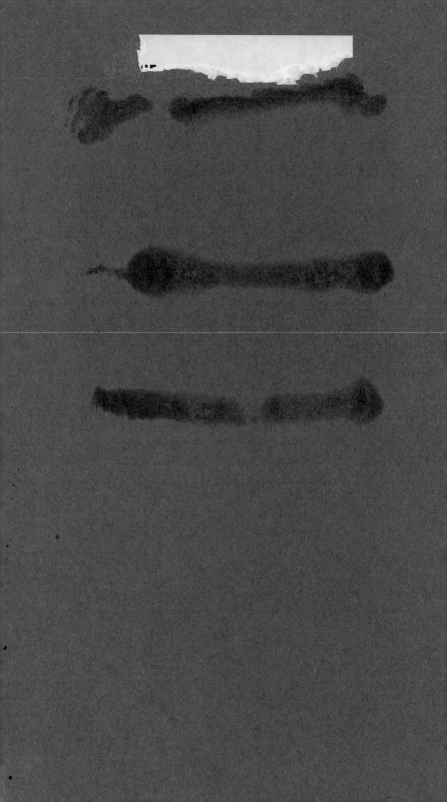